GW00871652

Performance Measurement in Financial Institutions in an ERM Framework

Performance Measurement in Financial Institutions in an ERM Framework

By Ashish Dev and Vandana Rao

Published by Risk Books, a Division of Incisive Financial Publishing Ltd

Haymarket House
28–29 Haymarket
London SW1Y 4RX
Tel: +44 (0)20 7484 9700
Fax: +44 (0)20 7484 9800
E-mail: books@incisivemedia.com
Sites: www.riskbooks.com
      www.incisivemedia.com

ISBN 1 904339 72 7

British Library Cataloguing in Publication Data
A catalogue record for this book is available from the British Library

Publisher: Laurie Donaldson
Assistant Editor: Steve Fairman
Designer: Rebecca Bramwell

Typeset by Mizpah Publishing Services Private Limited, Chennai, India

Printed and bound in Spain by Espacegrafic, Pamplona, Navarra

Conditions of sale

Contents

About the Authors

Ashish Dev is executive vice president at KeyCorp. As a member of ALCO and other high-level risk committees of KeyCorp, he is involved in decision making in all areas of risk (enterprise risk) in the bank. Ashish has been active in deliberations at all levels relating to Basel II. Under his direction, the efforts in operational risk in recent years in KeyCorp won an international *Operational Risk Achievement Award* in 2005. Ashish is listed as one of the most published authors in *Risk* magazine during the period 1994–2003. Prior to joining KeyCorp, he was head of quantitative research and analysis at Bank One. Ashish has a PhD in economics and holds the CFA professional designation.

Vandana Rao is associate professor of economics in the Business and Economics Division of Indiana University East. She teaches courses in finance, economics and statistics. Presently Vandana is also the coordinator of the online course offerings and program of the division. Vandana has won several teaching awards in the Indiana University system. Her research interests are diverse and range from economic demography to financial institutions. Vandana has worked as a research consultant/project director with community organisations at various levels, including UNICEF, the Government of India, and economic development agencies in the State of Indiana. Vandana has a PhD in economics.

Introduction

The simplest perception of enterprise risk management (ERM) is the management of all risks across an enterprise. We prefer to term this as *risk integration*, which is only part of the broader concept of enterprise risk management. Economic capital is often referred to as the common currency in which all risks arising from unexpected events are measured, thus enabling an integrated measurement of risk across the enterprise. No doubt economic capital is a measure of risk. But it is also the major driver of relatively new performance measures that align the objectives of managers in a financial institution with shareholder value enhancement. This *shareholder value creation* paradigm is obviously not limited to risk; it combines risk and return and spans across traditional risk and finance functions. Our concept of ERM is not one of risk management alone but follows the broader concept of a new *way of managing* a financial institution. This book treats various facets of performance measurement in a financial institution within this broad *ERM framework*.

As performance measurement in financial institutions moves progressively away from traditional measures and towards the objective of shareholder value creation, finance professionals need to understand the new drivers of performance. Risk professionals, on the other hand need to understand how measures of risk integrate with financial and operational drivers of the new measures of performance.

In the sprit of ERM, the book attempts to provide the readers an integral treatment of the three "legs" of internal performance measurement in a financial institution: *funds transfer pricing, economic capital* and *expense allocation*.

Chapter 1 is a modest compilation of traditional and risk-adjusted performance measures that are generally reported in the annual reports of most publicly traded financial institutions. Obviously these externally reported measures are at the corporate level rather than at the internal business unit level. The accounting and other principles that guide the measurement of such externally reported numbers are fairly uniform across financial institutions, at least within the US. Using illustrations from the 2005 annual report of a large and sophisticated US financial institution, we provide definitions for each of the performance measures. The definitions are perhaps already familiar to most of the readers but providing them at one place may be helpful to risk professionals and even some finance professionals, who are unfamiliar with external reporting on a day-to-day basis.

Internal business unit performance measurement, unlike externally reported performance measures, depends on internal methodologies. The three broad categories of internal methodologies that are critical to business unit performance measures are: *funds transfer pricing, economic capital allocation* and *expense allocation*. Although the concepts and basic methodologies of funds transfer pricing (FTP), economic capital and expense allocations are now fairly standardised across the financial institutions, in terms of details each institution can chose from among several possibilities, which will give somewhat different results. The internal methodologies need to be economically fair and generally transparent so that the business units, whose performances are being measured, view them as fair and objective.

In Chapter 2 we present the fundamentals of FTP. The primary purpose of FTP in a bank is to figure out the relative contributions of those engaged in gathering deposits and those engaged in lending money. Another objective of FTP is to isolate the computed revenues of business units in a bank from future fluctuations in interest rates. The FTP calculation has to be fundamentally consistent with the calculation of interest rate risk of the bank's book of business on the balance sheet. We discuss in details various aspects of the broad method of FTP called *matched funding*, which is the commonly used methodology in best practice financial institutions.

The derivation of the cost of funds curve from market observed interest rates, and computation of FTP rate using either the weighted average life method or using the full cash flow method have been provided in mathematical terms. The effect on FTP of specific characteristics of balance sheet transactions like prepayments, embedded options and basis risk have been discussed. A section of particular interest is devoted to the correct methodology for transfer pricing of equity or *equity crediting*.

Chapter 3 deals with the fundamentals of economic capital. The calculation of economic capital is mathematically more complex than that of FTP. In this chapter, we have avoided complex mathematics to provide a basic understanding of the concepts underlying economic capital. The chapter provides a method of computing the cost per unit of economic capital. It contrasts economic capital with regulatory capital and book equity. We have also introduced various applications of economic capital in a financial institution and have emphasised the significance of economic capital to managing a financial institution. Of the three legs of internal performance measurement, economic capital is by far the most unfamiliar to finance professionals. The correlation or portfolio diversification inherent in any economic capital calculation, which has a non-linear effect, is the most difficult concept to grasp. Economic capital has been the cornerstone of shareholder value creation paradigm in financial institutions. Managing a financial institution from the perspective of shareholder value creation requires non-traditional performance measures that are better aligned to share value.

Chapter 4 provides a broad overview of expense allocation. It is the third leg of internal performance measurement, which is probably the most familiar one to most finance professionals. Cost allocation is a common topic in accounting literature and we have not included many well-known aspects of costing in this chapter. We have focussed more on the role of expense allocation on internal performance measurement in a financial institution and on product pricing. Most financial institutions have introduced *activity based costing* (ABC) in the last decade as the fundamental methodology of expense allocation. A brief introduction to ABC has been provided in this chapter. The methodologies involved in both FTP and economic capital are analytically complex and relatively new. In contrast, expense allocation is analytically less challenging and has been in existence for a long time. Yet in terms of getting one's arms around it, the third leg is perhaps the most difficult. Risk professionals, particularly credit and market risk managers, in financial institutions are typically not familiar with the concepts introduced in this chapter.

Chapter 5 presents performance measurement of internal business units, bringing together the concepts of FTP, economic capital and expense allocation introduced in Chapters 2, 3 and 4 respectively. Contrasted with corporate measures (presented in Chapter 1), which are predicated by generally accepted accounting principles (GAAP), internal business unit performance measures also depend, often critically, on one or more internal methodology. This fact adds a whole new complexity not encountered while dealing with corporate performance measures. In this chapter we have tried to define precisely the more important financial performance measures used for internal performance measurement, monitoring and review. With the introduction of economic capital, the emphasis naturally gravitates towards risk-adjusted performance measures, aligned with the objective of shareholder value creation. Segment (public) reporting is a relatively new development in the financial industry. In the second part of the chapter we critically examine issues in segment reporting. Internal methodologies across financial institutions, though conceptually similar, may vary considerably in details. This is one reason why internal business unit performances across financial institutions may not be comparable. The other reason, which is a more serious issue, is that the way in which internal business units (with similar nomenclature) are organised may vary considerably from institution to institution. As a result it is dangerous to compare business unit performance across different financial institutions.

In Chapter 6 we examine details of risk-adjusted performance measurement and risk-based pricing of credit products and credit-based relationship. More and more financial institutions are looking upon a traditional loan product as an offering (at times as a loss leader) through which other financial products and services can be solicited to the customer, creating a multi-product/service relationship. Therefore, performance in general has to be looked upon from the perspective of single credit product as well as the perspective of a relationship. Part of the chapter deals with portfolio credit risk of various kinds of credit products and methodologies for calculating credit risk economic capital. Risk-based pricing takes a view of the lifetime of the product while internal risk-adjusted performance measurement takes a view of the contribution in a particular period (quarter or year). Risk-based pricing is specific to a vintage while risk-adjusted performance measurement is the contribution over all existing vintages. These distinctions have been discussed with specific reference to the possible confusion that may arise when the effects of these distinctions are not kept in mind.

Chapter 7 introduces active credit portfolio management (ACPM), a very new concept in financial institutions. Capital market credit instruments have only recently become available in meaningful ways for financial institutions in general to participate in ACPM strategies. The focus of the chapter is on how risk-adjusted performance can be enhanced through ACPM. In this chapter we provide a possible non-mathematical strategy for optimising or at least enhancing portfolio risk-adjusted return for all credits in general and portfolios of exposures to small and medium enterprises, in particular. In this chapter, we also introduce the concept of credit transfer pricing (CTP) and provide a mechanism of transfer pricing using economic capital as the basis. CTP creates a separation between the portfolio management and loan origination through which the possible conflict between the portfolio management and loan origination units can be resolved. We derive risk-adjusted performance measure(s) for the ACPM function. By focusing on this measure(s), the overall risk-adjusted performance of the financial institution can be significantly enhanced.

In Chapter 8 we go into details of FTP of indeterminate deposits. The depositor has the embedded option of withdrawing money in the account at any time with no penalty. Owing to the very fact that indeterminate deposits do not have a specified maturity or amortisation schedule, the methodologies of FTP introduced in Chapter 2 are very difficult to apply. Before applying the formulae in Chapter 2, it is necessary to model behaviour of balances of a portfolio of indeterminate deposit by product categories as well the movement of administered product rates paid to account holders. Since each portfolio consists of numerous individual accounts, the natural effect of law of large numbers makes modelling easier. In this chapter we provide an elaborate and slightly dull methodology for modelling indeterminate deposits with a detailed numerical example. The objective of such modelling is to derive the funds transfer credit to be given to such deposits. The ultimate objective is to measure the performance/contribution of indeterminate deposits.

Chapter 9 is an introduction to budgeting, performance monitoring and incentive compensation. Most of the concepts in this chapter are quite familiar to finance professionals but not necessarily to risk professionals in a financial institution. The chapter focuses on the disadvantages of the budgeting process. In spite of all the disadvantages of budgeting/planning, it remains at the core of financial planning, performance monitoring and is very relevant to determination of incentive compensation in a financial institution.

Chapter 10 introduces (BSC); While middle level managers in financial institutions have long taken one or more measures of operational efficiency into account in day-to-day management, in most high level performance review discussions, financial performance relative to budget has been the focus. To take a *balanced* view of the company's performance, in addition to financial measures, we need to take into account measures drawn from three other *"perspectives"* of the business. The four perspectives are: financial perspective, customer perspective, internal business process perspective, innovation and learning perspective. The most critical element of implementation of a BSC is how it is cascaded down the organisation. The chapter provides illustrative BSCs for a financial institution both at the corporate level and at one level below. The chapter closes with a critical discussion on strategic thinking and the role that BSC can play in strategic management.

In Chapter 11 we look at the recent international accord called Basel II from the perspective of improved financial and operational performance instead of viewing it as a regulation. Basel II aligns regulatory capital closer to economic capital. In doing so, its requirements force a bank to focus on relevant data and analytics as main drivers of risk measurement and management. Economic capital is at the core of new financial performance measures that are better aligned to shareholder value creation. Basel II almost created a whole new field of operational risk. The elements of Basel II advanced approach in operational risk are now the best practice in operational risk management, some of which can be used for process improvement and operational process efficiency. In this chapter we introduce the idea of *analytics based strategies*. The data requirements of Basel II coupled with customer relationship management tools can pave the way for such strategies which, if well executed, can give a financial institution a distinct competitive advantage.

From Traditional to Risk-Adjusted Measures of Corporate Level Performance

INTRODUCTION

Readers of this book are perhaps very familiar with balance sheet and income statement components of annual reports of public corporations in general and banks in particular. There is nothing new that is being presented in this chapter relating to traditional financial measures. The purpose is to define precisely the more important financial performance measures as they appear in extracts of the annual report for the year 2005 of a large US financial institution.

In recent years, leading financial institutions have started reporting risk-adjusted performance measures in their annual reports. It has always been recognised that in a financial institution, revenues and profits are generated by taking financial risk. But until the development of the concept of economic capital, there was no consistent way of measuring all kinds of risk quantitatively. Ironically, however, reporting risk-adjusted measures has resulted more from the imperative of creation of shareholder value than the recognition that return and risk go hand in hand. The risk-adjusted performance measures reported are generally variants of the concept of economic value added (EVA). The concept was originally introduced by the economist Alfred Marshall in the 1890s, applied in General Motors in the 1920s, discussed at length by the management guru Peter Drucker (Drucker, 1964) and popularised by Stern-Stewart in the 1980s. The introduction of economic capital in the 1990s was needed in order to compute something like EVA in a financial institution (see Chapter 3 on the Fundamentals of Economic Capital for more details).

This chapter is only concerned with corporate performance reported publicly or to a lender and not with internal performance measurement. Shareholder value creation for a public corporation over a period can be measured by taking into account dividends paid and change in market value of shares, which are both readily observable. Why then do we need a separate measure for shareholder value creation?

There is only one share price for the corporation. The managers of various functions or units of a financial institution do not have full (or much) control over the share price of the corporation. In order to make the internal performance measurement whose drivers are primarily controlled by the unit in question and yet consistent with and contributing to shareholder value of the corporation, we need a measure that satisfies both. EVA has been shown to be much better aligned with shareholder value than any traditional financial measure (see Uyemura *et al* 1996).

INCOME STATEMENT RELATED MEASURES

The primary function of a financial institution is financial intermediation. Financial intermediation, in its basic form, refers to borrowing funds from one group (of individuals typically) at one rate and lending funds to another group (of businesses typically) at a different rate. The financial intermediary makes money by creating a "spread gap" between the borrowing and lending rates. It is no surprise, therefore, that two of the oldest performance measures for a financial institution are *net interest income* and *net interest margin*.

Net interest income

$$NII = Interest\_Income - Interest\_expense$$
$$NII = Spread\_Income - Cost_{debt}$$

Net interest margin

$$NIM = \frac{NII}{Assets}$$

Figure 1 is an extract from the 2005 annual report of a large US financial institution. It shows the corresponding performance measures for the two preceding years as well. The NII for the year 2005 is US$13.9 billion.

Figure 1 Summaries of income

(In millions, except per share)	2005	2004	2003
Interest income	US$23,689	17,288	15,080
Tax-equivalent adjustment	219	250	256
Interest income	23,908	17,538	15,336
Interest expense	**10,008**	**5,327**	**4,473**
Net interest income	**13,900**	**12,211**	**10,863**

Figure 2 Summary of result of operation

(In millions, except per share)	2005	2004	2003
Net interest income (GAAP)	US$13,681	11,961	10,607
Tax-equivalent adjustment	219	250	256
Net interest income	**13,900**	**12,211**	**10,863**
Fee and other income	**12,219**	**10,779**	**9,482**
Total revenue	**26,119**	**22,990**	**20,345**
Provision for credit losses	249	257	586
Other noninterest expense	15,139	13,791	12,319
Merger-related and restructuring expenses	292	444	443
Other intangible amortisation	416	431	518
Total noninterest expense	**15,847**	**14,666**	**13,280**
Minority interest in income of consolidated subsidiaries	342	184	143
Income taxes	3,033	2,419	1,833
Tax-equivalent adjustment	219	250	256
Income from continuing operations before cumulative effect of a change in accounting principle	6,429	5,214	4,247
Discontinued operations, net of income taxes	214	–	–
Income before cumulative effect of a change in accounting principle	6,643	5,214	4,247
Cumulative effect of a change in accounting principle, net of income taxes	–	–	17
Net income	**6,643**	**5,214**	**4,264**
Dividends on preferred stock	–	–	5
Net income available to common stockholders	US$6,643	5,214	4,259
Diluted earnings per common share from continuing operations	US$4.05	3.81	3.18
Diluted earnings per common share available to common stockholders	**US$4.19**	**3.81**	**3.18**

Total revenue

Total revenue or simple *Revenue* is just the sum of net interest income and fee income.

$$Revenue = Net\_Interest\_Income + Fee\_Income$$

Figure 2 is another extract from the 2005 annual report of the same financial institution. The total revenue for the year 2005 is US$26,199 million.

Some institutions may define revenue in a gross sense, just like an industrial organisation, as the sum of interest income and fee income.[1]

Net income

In order to explicitly introduce taxes, before we define the most familiar traditional accounting measure "net income", we introduce earnings before tax:

$$EBT = Revenue - Non\_Interest\_Expense$$

or equivalently,

$$EBT = Int\_Income + Fee\_Income - Cost_{debt} - Exp_{direct} - Losses - Exp_{overhead}$$

where interest income has been abbreviated as Int_Income and Exp refer to expenses.

We can now define net income as:

$$NI = EBT - Taxes\_Paid$$

or

$$NI = (1 - \tau) * EBT$$

where τ is the effective tax rate.

Earnings per share

If S is the number of shares outstanding, then earnings per share is defined as:

$$eps = \frac{NI}{S}$$

In Figure 2, the (diluted) earnings per share in the year 2005 is US$4.19/share. Diluted eps is adjusted according to certain Generally Accepted Accounting Principles (GAAP) to arrive at reported earnings per share. Figure 3 is another extract from the 2005 Annual Report of the same financial institution.

We had introduced net interest margin and effective tax rate in the discussions above. The extract at Figure 4 shows that in the year 2005, NIM is 3.24% or 324 basis points and the effective tax rate was 32.05%.

Figure 3 Dividend payout ratios on common shares

	2005	2004	2005
Diluted earnings per common share *(GAAP)*	US$4.19	3.81	3.18
Other intangible amortisation	0.17	0.20	0.24
Merger-related and restructuring expenses	0.11	0.14	0.19
Discontinued operations *(GAAP)*	(0.14)	–	–
Cumulative effect of a change in accounting principle	–	–	(0.01)
Earnings per share	**US$1.33**	**4.15**	**3.60**
Dividends paid per common share	US$1.94	1.66	1.25
Dividend payout ratios *(GAAP)*	46.30%	43.57	39.31
Dividend payout ratios	44.80	40.00	34.72

Figure 4 Profitability

(Dollars in millions, except per share data)	2005	2004	2003
Net interest margin	3.24	3.41	3.72
Fee and other income as percentage of total revenue	46.78	46.88	46.61
Effective income tax rate	32.05	31.7	30.16

Expense ratio

Most finance professionals in financial institutions seem to devote considerable attention to expense or cost reduction. In this regard, the most common performance measure at the corporate level is the expense ratio:

$$Expense\_Ratio = \frac{Exp_{direct} + Exp_{overhead}}{Revenue}$$

BALANCE SHEET RELATED MEASURES

Figure 5 is another extract from the 2005 annual report of the same financial institution, representing the balance sheet. The total assets of the company at year-end 2005 were US$520,755 million. The total stockholders' equity at year-end 2005 was US$47,561 million. This is referred to as *book equity* (to distinguish it from *market value of equity* and *economic value of equity*, to be introduced later in the chapter).

Equity multiplier

The ratio of book value of assets to book value of equity is referred to as the equity multiplier.

$$Equity\_Multiplier = \frac{Book\_Value\_Assets}{Book\_Value\_Equity}$$

In the extract at Figure 5, the equity multiplier at year-end 2005 was 10.95. The average equity multiplier for the year 2005 was 10.83.

A ratio measure that is similar to the equity multiplier is the tangible equity to tangible assets ratio. Rating agencies, particularly Moody's, pays considerable attention to this ratio in rating the debt of a financial institution.

Tangible equity to tangible asset ratio

When intangible assets, goodwill and assets generally categorised as "other" assets are subtracted from total assets, the net figure is called *tangible assets*.

$$Tangible\_Equity\_Ratio = \frac{Tangible\_Equity}{Tangible\_Assets}$$

For a financial institution, it is important to distinguish between *earning* or *financial assets* and *liabilities* and *other assets* and *liabilities*. The earning assets and interest-bearing liabilities are shown in another extract of the same annual report in Figure 6. Figure 6 provides a break-up of earning assets and interest-bearing liabilities by categories and the corresponding interest margin.

Earning assets to core deposits ratio

Core deposits are considered more stable sources of funding for a commercial bank. The ability to raise core deposits often commands a premium in stock valuation. A measure of this is the loan to deposit ratio defined as follows:

$$Loan\_Deposit\_ratio = \frac{Earning\_assets}{Core\_deposits}$$

Figure 5 Consolidated balance sheet

(In millions, except per share data)	2005	2004
Assets		
Cash and due from banks	US$15,072	11,714
Interest-bearing bank balances	2,638	4,441
Federal funds sold and securities purchased under resale agreements (carrying amount of collateral held US$10,639 at December 31, 2005, US$1,290 repledged)	19,915	22,436
Total cash and cash equivalents	37,625	38,591
Trading account assets	42,704	45,932
Securities (amortized cost US$115,404 in 2005; US$108,835 in 2004)	114,889	110,597
Loans, net of unearned income (US$9,260 in 2005; US$9,699 in 2004)	259,015	223,840
Allowance for loan losses	(2,724)	(2,757)
Loans, net	256,291	221,083
Loans held for sale	6,405	12,988
Premises and equipment	4,910	5,268
Due from customers on acceptances	824	718
Goodwill	21,807	21,526
Other intangible assets	1,208	1,581
Other assets	34,092	35,040
Total assets	**US$520,755**	**493,324**
Liabilities and stockholders' equity		
Deposits		
Noninterest-bearing deposits	67,487	64,197
Interest-bearing deposits	257,407	230,856
Total deposits	**324,894**	**295,053**
Short-term borrowings	61,953	63,406
Bank acceptances outstanding	892	755
Trading account liabilities	17,598	21,709
Other liabilities	15,986	15,507
Long-term debt	48,971	46,759
Total liabilities	**470,294**	**443,189**
Minority interest in net assets of consolidated subsidiaries	2900	2,818
Stockholders' equity		
Preferred stock, Class A, 40 million shares, no par value; 10 million shares, no par value; none issued	–	–
Dividend Equalisation Preferred shares, no par value, outstanding 97 million shares in 2005 and in 2004	–	–
Common stock, US$3.33-1/3 par value; authorised 3 billion shares, outstanding 1.557 billion shares in 2005; 1.588 billion shares in 2004	5,189	5,294
Paid-in capital	31,172	31,120
Retained earnings	11,973	10,178
Accumulated other comprehensive income, net	773	725
Total stockholders' equity	**47,561**	**47,317**

Figure 6 Average balance sheet and interest rate

(In millions)	2005		2004	
	Average Balances	Interest Rate	Average Balances	Interest Rate
Interest-bearing bank balances	US$2,516	3.23%	US$3,578	1.43%
Federal funds sold	24,008	3.31	24,940	1.37
Trading account assets	33,800	4.94	28,944	4.28
Securities	115,107	5.14	100,960	4.90
Commercial loans, net	132,504	5.69	99,026	4.63
Consumer loans, net	95,418	5.81	73,007	5.24
Total loans, net	227,922	5.74	172,033	4.89
Loans held for sale	15,293	5.71	16,735	4.42
Other earning assets	9,944	5.36	11,064	3.30
Risk management derivatives	–	0.23	–	0.41
Total earning assets	**428,590**	**5.58**	**358,254**	**4.90**
Interest-bearing deposits	242,152	2.00	196,142	1.12
Federal funds purchased	54,302	3.08	47,321	1.35
Commercial paper	11,898	3.05	12,034	1.35
Securities sold short	10,279	3.31	11,025	2.88
Other short-term borrowings	6,675	1.87	6,087	0.90
Long-term debt	47,774	4.46	39,780	4.00
Risk management derivatives	–	0.14	–	0.12
Total interest-bearing liabilities	**373,080**	**2.68**	**312,389**	**1.71**
Net interest income and margin	**US$13,900**	**3.24%**	**US$12,211**	**3.41%**

Figure 7 Deposits

(In millions)	2005	2004	2005
Core deposits			
Noninterest-bearing	US$67,487	64,197	48,683
Savings and NOW accounts	81,536	83,678	63,011
Money market accounts	100,220	91,184	65,045
Other consumer time	44,319	35,529	27,921
Total core deposits	**293,562**	**274,588**	**204,660**
Other deposits			
Foreign	18,041	9,881	9,151
Other time	13,291	10,584	7,414
Total deposits	**US$324,894**	**295,053**	**221,225**

PERFORMANCE RATIOS RELATING TO BOTH THE B/S AND THE I/S

For purposes of comparison across different financial institutions, the income statement and balance sheet related financial perform-ance measures are less used than certain performance ratios that

Figure 8 Performance ratios

	2005	2004	2003
Assets to stockholders' equity	10.83X	12.09	11.25
Return on assets	**1.31%**	**1.22**	**1.18**
Return on common stockholders' equity	14.13	14.77	13.25
Return on total stockholders' equity	**14.13%**	**14.77**	**13.27**

pertain to both. The most common of these performance ratios are return on assets and return on equity. It is also instructive to relate such ratio measures to other ratios through a Dupont analysis. Appendix 1 provides such a diagram, which has been adapted from Saunders and Cornett (2003).

Return on assets

Return on assets (ROA) is simply the net income in the year divided by total assets, usually the average value over the year instead of year-end book value of assets.

$$ROA = \frac{NI}{Average\_Total\_Assets}$$

Figure 8 is another extract from the 2005 annual report which contains the performance ratios. It shows that the ROA for 2005 was 1.31%.

Return on book equity

As financial institutions' business model moved away from pure intermediation, the traditional financial measure that has become perhaps the most important is return on equity. Here the term book equity is used deliberately to distinguish this traditional account-ing measure from risk-adjusted measures that will be introduced.

$$RO(book)E = \frac{NI}{Book\_Equity}$$

In Figure 8, the reported ROE for 2005 is 14.13%.

MARKET-RELATED MEASURES

In this section, market refers to the equity capital markets. Valuation in the equity market are determined both by the fundamentals in

Figure 9 Selected statistical data

(Dollars in millions, except per share data)	2005	2004	2003
FTE employees	93,980	96,030	86,114
Total financial centres/brokerage offices	3,850	3,971	3,328
ATMs	5,119	5,321	4,408
Registered common stockholders	177,924	185,647	170,205
Actual common shares *(In millions)*	1,557	1,588	1,312
Common stock price	US$52.86	52.60	46.59
Market capitalisation	US$82,291	83,537	61,139

the income statement and the balance sheet and by many other factors including investor psychology.

Market capitalisation
Market capitalisation is simply the number of shares outstanding S multiplied by the current share price by P:

$$Market\_Cap = P * S$$

Market capitalisation can also be referred to as market value of equity. In the extract of the 2005 annual report shown in Figure 9, the market capitalisation for the financial institution as of December 31, 2005 was US$82.3 billion.

Price earnings ratio
Conceptually, the price to earning ratio reflects the future growth opportunities of *eps* reflected in the current stock price. It is defined as:

$$P/E\_Ratio = \frac{P}{eps}$$

The 2005 year-end stock price was US$52.86 and the *eps* for the year 2005 was US$4.19, resulting in a *P/E* of 12.62.

Market to book ratio
Another measure of future growth opportunities reflected in the stock price is what is known as the market to book ratio also referred to as Tobin's Q:

$$Tobin's\_Q = \frac{Market\_Cap}{Book\_Equity}$$

Figure 10 Per common share data

(Dollars in millions, except per share data)	2005	2004	2003
Basic			
Income from continuing operations before change in accounting principle	US$4.13	3.87	3.2
Net income	4.27	3.87	3.21
Diluted			
Income from continuing operations before change in accounting principle	4.05	3.81	3.17
Net income	4.19	3.81	3.18
Cash dividends	US$1.94	1.66	1.25
Average common shares – Basic	1,556	1,346	1,325
Average common shares – Diluted	1,585	1,370	1,340
Average common stockholders' equity	**US$47,019**	**35,295**	**32,135**
Book value per common share	30.55	29.79	24.71
Common stock price			
High	56.01	54.52	46.59
Low	46.49	43.56	32.72
Year-end	**US$52.86**	**52.6**	**46.59**
To earnings ratio	**12.62X**	**13.81**	**14.65**
To book value	**173%**	**177**	**189**

At year-end 2005, the market to book ratio for the financial institution was 1.73 as seen at the end of Figure 10.

RISK-RELATED TRADITIONAL MEASURES
Asset quality has for long been a topic of interest with analysts looking at a commercial bank's performance. By far the biggest risk in as commercial bank is usually credit risk. The two traditional measures of *credit risk* reflecting asset quality are net charge-off and NPL ratio.

Net charge-off
Loans that are not accruing the necessary coupon and principal payments are charged-off. The outstanding principal is the nominal amount, often referred to as "gross charge-off" but part of the principal is usually recovered even for unsecured loans. Hence the term "net". Net charge-off can be expressed as a dollar amount or as a percentage of all loan balances.

Figure 11 Asset quality

(In millions)	2005	2004	2003
Loans, net	US$259,015	223,840	165,571
Allowance for loan losses	US$2,724	2,757	2,348
Allowance as % of loans, net	1.05%	1.23	1.42
Allowance as % of non-accrual and restructured loans	439	289	227
Allowance as % of nonperforming assets	378%	251	205
Net charge-offs	US$207	300	652
Net charge-offs as % of average loans, net	0.09%	0.17	0.41
Nonperforming assets			
Non-accrual loans	US$620	955	1,035
Foreclosed properties	100	145	111
Loans held for sale	32	157	82
Total nonperforming assets	US$752	1,257	1,228
Nonperforming assets to loans, net, foreclosed properties and loans held for sale	0.28%	0.53	0.69

$$NCO(\%) = \frac{Balance\_of\_Loans\_charged\_off}{Balance\_of\_All\_Loans}$$

Nonperforming loans ratio

$$NPL\_Ratio = \frac{Balance\_of\_Non\_performing\_Loans}{Balance\_of\_All\_Loans}$$

Figure 11 shows the average NPL ratio for the year 2005 to be a low 0.28%.

Unfortunately, neither NPL nor NCO over a period tells us much about the credit performance of the institution's portfolios in the future.

Earnings at risk

Scenarios of interest rate curves are created, one reflecting upward movement and another reflecting downward movement (usually mirror images of each other). The interest and principal cash flows from assets and liabilities under each of these scenarios are computed. The earnings over the next 12 months are calculated (without discounting within the one year period) for each of these

Figure 12 Policy period sensitivity measurement

	Actual fed funds rate at 1-Jan-06	Implied fed funds rate at 31-Dec-06	Percent earnings sensitivity
Market forward rate scenarios	4.26%	4.64	–
High rate composite		6.64	(1.50)
Low rate		2.64	1.70

scenarios in addition to a base scenario, typically defined as the current rates or some consensus forecast.

The following is defined:

$$\Delta E_{up} = Earnings_{up\_scenario} - Earnings_{base\_scenario}$$
$$\Delta E_{down} = Earnings_{down\_scenario} - Earnings_{base\_scenario}$$
$$\Delta EAR_{up/down} = \frac{\Delta E_{up/down}}{Earnings_{base\_scenario}}$$

In Figure 12, EAR is a *negative* 1.50% in the high rate (up) scenario. This implies that the balance sheet position is such that earnings over the next 12 months may fall by 1.50% owing to interest rate risk. EAR is a short-term interest rate risk measure and ignores the effect on cash flows in the long-term.

Duration of equity

The assets and liabilities in the balance sheet of a financial institution are not marked to market. Accounting rules require accrual accounting for assets and liabilities. More importantly, most of these assets and liabilities do not have a liquid market where the prices can be readily observed. However, asset liability management typically simulates the interest and principal cash flows for different interest rate scenarios. The present value of the cash flows of assets and liabilities can be computed. Economic value of equity is the difference between the present value of the asset cash flows and the present value of liability cash flows.

$$EVE = PV(cashflows\_assets) - PV(cashflows\_liabilities)$$

The reader may note that economic value of equity is different from market value of equity, which in turn is different from the book value of equity. The sources and methodologies of the valuations for these three different measures are indeed different and one cannot expect them to be equal, even approximately.

The present values of the cash flows of assets and liabilities can also be computed for an instantaneous increase in all rates by Δr and an instantaneous decrease in all rates by Δr. Using the economic values of equity so calculated, the duration of equity can be defined just as we define duration of a bond.[2]

$$Dur\_Equity = -\frac{1}{2*\Delta r} * \frac{[EVE_{up} - EVE_{down}]}{EVE}$$

The rate changes in the up and down scenarios for calculating EAR are typically not instantaneous shocks, whereas those for computing duration of equity are by definition. Duration calculation takes all future cash flows into account and discounts them, while EAR is concerned with cash flows in the next 12 months, ignoring discounting.

RISK-ADJUSTED PERFORMANCE MEASURES

As indicated in the previous section, traditional measures of performance did include measures of risk. But by the very nature of the traditional measures, they tell us very little of the institution's

Figure 13 Liquidity risk management

(In millions)	Total	One year or Less	Over one year through three years	Over three years through five years	Over five years
Contractual Commitments (December 31, 2005)					
Deposit maturities	US$324,894	304,660	15,170	4,599	465
Long-term debt	48,971	8,826	16,833	5,337	17,975
Operating lease obligations	4,540	592	1,071	903	1,974
Capital lease obligations	18	3	6	4	5
Investment obligations	817	817	–	–	–
Other purchase obligations	980	783	161	36	–
Total	**US$380,220**	**315,681**	**33,241**	**10,879**	**20,419**

portfolio risk behaviour. In industry parlance, risk-adjusted performance measure has become synonymous with performance measure that takes economic capital into account.

Total economic capital (EC)

Economic capital is formally defined as the potential unexpected (dollar) loss of economic value over one year calculated at a pre-specified confidence level. The level of confidence is anchored by the desired insolvency standard of the financial institution. Less formally, economic capital is a dollar number that serves as a common measure across all types of financial risks and captures the risk of unexpected losses or unexpected reductions in income in a business, a portfolio or a single transaction. Whereas economic capital for some specific portfolio can be computed relatively accurately, total economic capital for a multi-line financial institution cannot yet be measured with dependable accuracy. This is because no one really knows accurately the inter-portfolio correlation between one type of business and another – a very important determinant of total economic capital. Therefore, the total economic capital number reported by a financial institution has to be considered as approximate.

Figure 15 shows the total economic capital to be US$16,932 million, average over the year 2005. Even though economic capital is the common currency in which all risks are expressed, generally economic capital is reported for three major risk categories: (a) EC for credit risk; (b) EC for market risk; and (c) EC for operational risk. In the extract from the 2005 Annual Report, the lower portion of Figure 15 provides a short description of what constitutes each of three broad categories and indicates that credit risk represents 53% of the total economic capital, market risk (including balance sheet interest rate risk) represents 23% and operational risk represents 24%.

For the trading portfolio, a more common measure of market risk, however, is *value-at-risk.*

Value-at-risk

Value-at-risk is defined as the potential loss of value of a *trading* portfolio over a specified horizon (usually one day) calculated at a pre-specified confidence level (usually 95%). Trading portfolios are marked to market, unlike the assets and liabilities in the bank book or "accrual" book.

Figure 14 VAR profile by risk type

(In millions)	2005			2004		
Risk category	High	Low	Avg	High	Low	Avg
Interest rate	US$25.9	10.0	15.1	20.3	4.7	12.4
Foreign exchange	2.1	0.2	0.8	3.0	0.2	1.2
Equity	16.2	5.6	10.4	20.0	6.2	10.7
Commodity	1.3	0.1	0.5	0.9	–	0.2
Aggregate	**US$28.4**	**11.9**	**19.2**	**27.4**	**11.8**	**18.7**

Return on risk-adjusted capital (RORAC)

Since economic capital is a measure of risk, it is already risk-adjusted. The ratio of net income to economic capital is essentially a return on risk-adjusted capital or RORAC:

$$RAROC = \frac{NI}{EC}$$

Return on risk-adjusted capital (RORAC) and risk-adjusted return on capital (RAROC) are often used interchangeably. However, this chapter makes a purposeful distinction by defining RAROC as follows.

Risk-adjusted return on capital (RAROC)

$$RAROC = \frac{NI - k * EC}{EC}$$

where k is the institution's cost of equity or required return on equity (see Chapter 3 as to how k is determined).

Economic profit (EP)

Economic profit or economic value added (EVA) or shareholder value added (SVA) as it is variously known, The concept was originally introduced by the economist Alfred Marshall in the 1890s, applied in General Motors in the 1920s, discussed at length by the management guru Peter Drucker (Drucker 1964) and popularised by Stern-Stewart in the 1980s. It gained acceptance in the financial industry in the 1990s.

$$EP = NI - k * EC$$

or more generally,

$$EP = Revenue - Expenses - Taxes - EL - k * EC$$

Figure 15 Consolidated financial statement

(Dollars in millions)	2005	2004	2003
Net interest income	US$13,681	11,961	10,607
Fee and other income	12,219	10,779	9,482
Intersegment revenue	–	–	–
Total revenue	25,900	22,740	20,089
Provision for credit losses	249	257	586
Noninterest expense	15,847	14,666	13,280
Minority interest	342	184	143
Income taxes (benefits)	3,033	2,419	1,833
Tax-equivalent adjustment	–	–	–
Income before cumulative effect of a change in accounting principle	–	–	4,247
Cumulative effect of a change in accounting principle, net of income taxes	–	–	17
Net income	–	–	4,264
Dividends on preferred stock	–	–	5
Income from continuing operations	6,429	–	–
Discontinued operations, net of income taxes	214	–	–
Net income available to common stockholders	US$6,643	5,214	4,259
Economic profit	**US$4,668**	**3,816**	**2,998**
Risk-adjusted return on capital	**38.57%**	**37.82**	**30.87**
Economic capital, average	**US$16,932**	**14,226**	**15,088**
Cash overhead efficiency ratio	57.96%	59.98	60.55
Lending commitments	US$220,837	180,307	139,679
Average loans, net	227,922	172,033	158,327
Average core deposits	US$278,721	231,608	183,122
FTE employees	93,980	96,030	86,114

The types of risk to which we attribute economic capital are:

❑ *Credit risk*: Credit risk, which represented *53% of our economic capital in 2005*, is the risk of loss due to adverse changes in a borrower's ability to meet its financial obligations under agreed-upon terms.

❑ *Market risk*: The major components of market risk, which represented *23% of economic capital*, are interest rate risk inherent in the balance sheet, price risk in the principal investing portfolio and market value risk in the trading portfolios.

❑ *Operational, business and other risk*: Operational risk is the risk of loss from inadequate or failed internal processes, people and systems or from external events. This risk is inherent in all the businesses. Business risk is the potential losses the business lines could suffer that have not been captured elsewhere (such as losses from a difficult business environment). Business and operational risk capital are the primary types of capital held by non-balance sheet intensive businesses such as trust, asset management and brokerage. Other risk represents the loss in value that other miscellaneous and fixed assets could realise that are not captured as market risk. Operational, business and other risk represented *24% of economic capital in 2005*.

Figure 16 Summary of off-balance sheet

(In millions)	Carrying Amount	Exposure
Guarantees		
Securities and other lending indemnifications	US$ –	62,597
Standby letters of credit	108	35,568
Liquidity agreements	8	27,193
Loans sold with recourse	47	9,322
Residual value guarantees	–	1,344
Total guarantees	US$163.00	136,024

(In millions)	December 31, 2005			
	2005		2004	
	Notional amount	Estimated fair value	Notional amount	Estimated fair value
Off-balanace sheet financial instruments				
Lending commitments	US$215,353	310	170,818	316
Standby letters of credit	35,568	108	30,815	101
Financial guarantees written	US$100,456	55	64,314	49

PERFORMANCE OF OFF-BALANCE SHEET ACTIVITIES

Most large financial institutions engage in positions in financial instruments that are considered off-balance sheet activities under current accounting rules. The most common off-balance sheet activities are lines of credit, securitisation, servicing of loans – whether originated by the institution or not, positions in derivative instruments like interest rate swaps, options, caps and floors etc.

The income or profit and loss generated by the off-balance sheet positions are included in the income statement. But they are not parts of assets or liabilities in the balance sheet. As a result, if the size of the off-balance sheet activities is considerable, then the traditional performance ratios can be distorted in significant ways.

Off-balance sheet activities also introduce risk, which is not very well captured in the traditional measures. Economic capital calculations make no distinction whether a portfolio is accounted for in the balance sheet or off-balance sheet.

Figure 17 Loans – on-balance sheet, and managed and servicing portfolios

(In millions)	2005	2004	2003
On-balance sheet loan portfolio			
commercial			
Commercial, financial and agricultural	US$87,327	75,095	55,453
Real estate – construction and other	13,972	12,673	5,969
Real estate – mortgage	19,966	20,742	15,186
Lease financing	25,368	25,000	23,978
Foreign	10,221	7,716	6,880
Total commercial	156,854	141,226	107,466
Consumer			
Real estate secured	94,748	74,161	50,726
Student loans	9,922	10,468	8,435
Installment loans	6,751	7,684	8,965
Total consumer	111,421	92,313	68,126
Total loans	268,275	233,539	175,592
Unearned income	9,260	9,699	10,021
Loans, net *(On-balance sheet)*	US$259,015	223,840	165,571
Managed portfolio commercial			
On-balance sheet loan portfolio	US$156,854	141,226	107,466
Securitised loans – off-balance sheet	1,227	1,734	2,001
Loans held for sale	3,860	2,112	2,574
Total commercial	161,941	145,072	112,041
Consumer			
Real estate secured			
On-balance sheet loan portfolio	94,748	74,161	50,726
Securitised loans – off-balance sheet	8,438	7,570	8,897
Securitised loans included in securities	4,817	4,838	10,905
Loans held for sale	2,296	10,452	9,618
Total real estate secured	110,299	97,021	80,146
Student			
On-balance sheet loan portfolio	9,922	10,468	8,435
Securitised loans – off-balance sheet	2,000	463	1,658
Securitised loans included in securities	52	–	–
Loans held for sale	–	128	433
Total student	11,974	11,059	10,526
Installment			
On-balance sheet loan portfolio	6,751	7,684	8,965
Securitised loans – off-balance sheet	3,392	2,184	–
Securitised loans included in securities	206	195	–
Loans held for sale	249	296	–
Total instalment	10,598	10,359	8,965
Total consumer	132,871	118,439	99,637
Total managed portfolio	US$294,812	263,511	211,678
Servicing portfolio			
Commercial	US$173,428	136,578	85,693
Consumer	US$56,741	38,442	13,279

CONCLUSION

The large number of traditional and non-traditional corporate performance measures presented in this chapter constitutes all the tangible items that are available to investors and analysts for gauging the health of a financial institution. While a lot can be inferred from these reported measures, they do not provide a good picture of the composition of a financial institution's portfolios of financial instruments, particularly in terms of the risk characteristics. This is at the root of the Pillar 3 provisions of the recent Basel II Accord, which requires considerable disclosure in a common format about the risk characteristics of the institution's portfolios.

The financial performance measures reported also do not throw much light on productivity (however measured) improvement. This statement is true of reported performance measures of non-financial corporations as well. Yet for any sector, productivity is the most important determinant of future growth and profitability, productivity resulting from two dimensions – knowledge and innovation (see Drucker, 1993).

More than most other industries, financial institutions have undergone immense changes in the utilisation of information technology and customer information in the last two decades and have also seen unprecedented growth of new innovative products. In almost all investor relations dialogues, neither the financial institution nor the bank analysts dwells on issues of productivity and even less so on product innovation. It is difficult to imagine how quality analysis can be done with the performance measures reported by financial institutions – with information about portfolio composition, productivity measures and R&D (in this case product or delivery innovation) missing.

APPENDIX 1

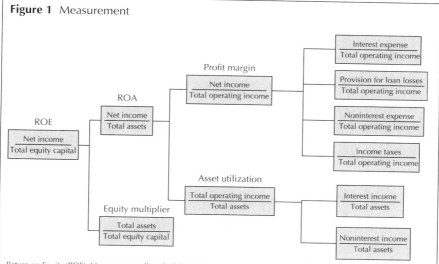

Figure 1 Measurement

Return on Equity (ROE): Measures overall profitability of the financial institution per dollar of equity.

Return on Assets (ROA): Measures profit generated relative to the financial institution's assets.

Equity Multiplier (EM): Measures the extent to which assets of the financial institution are funded with equity relative to debt.

Profit Margin (PM): Measure the ability to pay expenses and generate net income from interest and noninterest income.

Asset Utilisation (AU): measure the amount of interest and noninterest income generated per dollar of total assets.

Adapted from Saunders and Cornett (2003)

APPENDIX 2: FOOTNOTE TO EARNINGS SENSITIVITY

Earnings Sensitivity The Policy Period Sensitivity Measurement table provides a summary of our interest rate sensitivity measurement.

Our model's forward rate expectations imply an additional 25 basis points to 50 basis points of tightening for the federal funds target rate by year-end 2006. If these expectations prove to be correct, the spread between the 10-year treasury note rate and the federal funds rate would compress from a positive 30 basis points of slope at December 31, 2005, to an inverted yield curve of negative 26 basis points of slope by year-end 2006. The current market expectations, therefore, do not reflect a yield curve shape consistent with a scenario where short-term rates rise an additional 200 basis points. Therefore, our high rate sensitivity to the "market forward rate" scenario is measured using three different yield curve shapes. These yield curves are constructed to represent the likely range of yield curve shapes that may prevail in an environment where short-term rates rise 200 basis points above current market expectations. The reported sensitivity is a composite of these three scenarios.

1   In banking, the term "income" is used somewhat ambiguously. It does not always have the pure connotation of revenue net of expense. Thus, when the term interest income is used, it is really a "revenue" connotation.

2   The analogy ends there. EVE and price of a bond behave very differently.

REFERENCES

Drucker, P. 1964, *Managing for Results*, New York: Harper and Row.

Drucker, P. 1993, "The New Organization," SEI Distinguished Lecture, The Wharton School, Philadelphia, April.

Saunders, A. and M. Cornett, 2003, *Financial Institutions: A Risk Management Perspective*, New York: McGraw Hill.

Uyemura, D. G., C. C. Cantor, and J. M. Pettit, 1996, EVA for Banks: Value Creation, Risk Management and Profitability Measurement, *Journal of Applied Corporate Finance,* **9(2)**, pp 94–113.

2

The Fundamentals of Funds Transfer Pricing

INTRODUCTION

The primary function of a financial institution is financial intermediation. Financial intermediation, in its basic form, refers to borrowing funds from one group (of individuals typically) at one rate and lending funds to another group (of businesses typically) at a different rate. The financial intermediary makes money by creating a "spread gap" between the borrowing and lending rates. But in reality, financial products used for both borrowing and lending are complex, often with contingent cash-flows and different maturities and amortisations. Thus calculating the "gap" is not simple.

From the perspective of day-to-day management, it is perhaps even more important for a bank to figure out the relative contributions of those engaged in gathering deposits and those engaged in lending money. This is the attribution of the "spread gap" created through intermediation to both the liability and the asset sides. The method by which this is achieved has come to be known as funds transfer pricing (FTP). Another objective of FTP is to isolate the computed revenues of business units in a bank from future fluctuations in interest rates. The interest rate risk is computed and managed at the corporate level, generally by the Treasury function. Treasury charges an FTP charge for each transaction on the asset side of the balance sheet and credits an FTP credit to each transaction on the liability side.

Funds transfer pricing is purely for internal performance measurement purposes. Therefore, from a market discipline perspective, a bank is free to use any method it wants. But for large banks under regulatory scrutiny, the FTP methodology must conform to industry best practice. Also to satisfy so many different constituents that get affected by the transfer price charged (or credited), the FTP methodology has to somewhat objective, transparent and rooted in some unambiguous market (interest rate) data. Finally, almost by definition, the FTP calculation has to be fundamentally consistent with the calculation of interest rate risk of the bank's book of business on the balance sheet.

BROAD METHODOLOGIES OF FTP

The simplest (though quite outdated by now) method of funds transfer pricing is to utilise a single FTP rate to charge all lenders and credit all fund gatherers. This method is known as the *single pool FTP* method. While it is easy to understand and implement, it does not take into consideration the differences in characteristics of many different assets and liabilities in the books of a modern financial institution. The *specific matching FTP* attempts to match every specific liability with every specific asset of an equal amount, maturity and amortisation. This method is only hypothetical because the assets and liabilities of a financial institution are never perfectly matched. A third transfer pricing method is *multiple pool matching FTP*. Essentially, each side of the balance sheet is split into pools of assets and liabilities related by criteria such as maturity characteristic, rate and yield, imbedded risk or credit factors. Then the pools from each side of the balance sheet are matched to the opposite side of the balance sheet to establish a related funds charge or credit.

A fourth broad method of transfer pricing is *matched maturity FTP* (sometimes referred to as simply *matched funding* or even as *coterminous FTP*). This is the preferred approach to FTP and is utilised in one form or other by sophisticated financial institutions and is offered by leading vendors of asset liability management/funds transfer pricing systems. In this chapter we will not go into FTP systems. The reader is referred to Chapter 26 of Bessis (2002). The sections that follow will only be describing the components and various ramifications of this fourth method of funds transfer pricing. For more details of the other three simpler methods of funds transfer pricing, the reader is referred to Kafafian (2001).

COST OF FUNDS

The opportunity cost of money is the market rate at which a bank can borrow or lend (transfer of principal) money. Of course, the cost will depend on point in time and also the term and the amortisation of principal repayments. Since most banks operate at a very high leverage ratio and not all debt is retail deposits, there is plenty of debt issuance by a bank in the wholesale market. The corporate (in this case bank) debt yield curve is commonly expressed as a spread over treasury yield curve or over the libor-swap yield curve. This spread increases with the term and also depends on the rating of the bank. This spread is referred to as credit spread or liquidity premium. The libor-swap market is one of the most liquid markets and the bid-ask spread is typically very small. Therefore, for all practical purposes using the same rate (say the mid point of the bid-ask spread or the "Limean"), whether it is for borrowing or lending, is not far off the mark. In what follows, we will use the libor-swap curve for convenience of notation but the same could have been done starting from the treasury yield curve.

We will refer to the FTP rate for each term point as the cost of funds (COF) Curve. From what has been described in the last paragraph, it follows that the FTP cost of funds consists of a Base FTP rate and a liquidity premium. First the COF curve will discussed for fixed rate assets and liabilities. The libor-swap yield curve is quoted for a limited number of term points. The accounting system in a bank is typically uses a month as the frequency of booking entries. Therefore, one needs to obtain the COF curve for each monthly term point. The methods of interpolation and bootstrapping so common to interest rate term structure modelling also applies to FTP calculation. This includes corrections for different conventions of quoting the libor rates below one year and swap rates beyond one year. All points of the yield curve are effectively converted to rates corresponding to monthly coupons. A detailed description of the concepts and methods of term structure modelling is beyond the scope of this chapter. The reader is referred to Fabozzi (2002). Let $t = 1, 2, \ldots$ represent the term points (months) at which the interpolated curve is calculated.

Even though entries are booked on a monthly basis, the FTP rate may be calculated and communicated on a daily, weekly or a monthly basis in a bank. In the same bank, there may be an FTP rate for each day for some products (eg, large institutional loans), for each week for some products (eg, mortgage lending) and for each month for some products (eg, indirect auto lending or indeterminate deposits). Therefore, beyond yield curve interpolation, an averaging of daily observed libor-swap yield curves over a week or a month is called for in FTP calculations. This averaging over a month is not to be confused with the monthly term points t.

The second component of the COF curve is the liquidity premium (LP). This depends on the credit rating of the bank. A bank with a double A rating will have a lower value of LP for every term point compared with a bank with a Triple B rating. The LP is zero for term points up to 12 months irrespective of the rating of the bank. It is common practice to recalculate LP less frequently than the base FTP rate. Thus the COF curve for a vintage τ

$$COF_\tau(t) = Base\ Rate_\tau(t) + LP_\tau(t) \qquad for\ t = 1, 2, \ldots \qquad \textbf{(1)}$$

The vintage is defined as the point in time (day, week or month as the case may be) at which the asset or liability is originated. COF curve of vintage τ is applied to the principal cash flows of all instruments originated during that vintage period.

Till now we have restricted ourselves to fixed-rate assets and liabilities. Over the years floating-rate assets and liabilities have grown in proportion to fixed-rate ones. The COF for a Floating-rate instrument is given by:

$$COF_\tau(t) = Short\ Rate + LP_\tau(t) \qquad for\ t = 1, 2, \ldots \qquad \textbf{(1a)}$$

FTP RATE CALCULATION BASED ON WEIGHTED AVERAGE LIFE

The FTP rate for any transaction depends on the amortisation schedule of the principal cash flows. One way of capturing the amortisation schedule is the measure called weighted average life (WAL). WAL calculation ignores the coupon cash flows of the transaction. If B_t represents the outstanding (principal) balance at time t, then the WAL is given by the formula:

$$WAL = \frac{1}{B_0} \sum_t (B_{t-1} - B_t) \cdot t \qquad \textbf{(2)}$$

The FTP rate for a fixed-rate instrument is then given by

$$f_\tau = COF_\tau(t = WAL) \tag{3}$$

For a floating-rate instrument,

$$f_\tau = Short\ Rate + LP_\tau(t = WAL) \tag{3a}$$

Note that the FTP rate for a fixed-rate instrument does not change over the life of the instrument, although the balance to which the FTP rate applies may vary from month to month. The FTP rate for a floating-rate instrument changes every month as the short rate changes.

FTP RATE CALCULATION BASED ON ALL CASH-FLOWS

The above method based on WAL is simple to implement and is a good approximation only when the yield curve is relatively flat. Since most of the time (vintage, in the current terminology), the yield curve is not flat, the simple method is not adequate. One needs to take into account all the principal cash flows at the times they occur and sink them with the appropriate points of the COF curve. In case of a bullet asset or liability this is simple. All the principal is repaid at maturity. Therefore, the only point in the COF curve that is relevant is the maturity term point. In the case of an amortising instruments (which is much more common than bullet instruments in a bank's balance sheet), it is a bit more complex. The balance that drops off in the time period from $t-1$ to t can be represented as $(B_{t-1} - B_t)$. This is the part of the original balance that had to be funded every month for a term of t. The total funding cost (accounting ignores time value of money) is $\Sigma_\tau[(B_{t-1} - B_t) \cdot t \cdot COF_\tau(t)]$. Keeping in line with the objective that the business unit's cash flows or more precisely, spread incomes in the future are immunised, one can find the single (time invariant) rate would give the same total funding cost. That is, $\Sigma_t f_\tau \cdot [(B_{t-1} - B_t) \cdot t]$ is equated to the earlier expression to derive the FTP rate as:

$$f_\tau = \sum_t [(B_{t-1} - B_t) \cdot t \cdot COF_\tau(t)] \Big/ \sum_t [(B_{t-1} - B_t) \cdot t] \tag{4}$$

In the above expression, $COF_\tau(t)$ may be given by Equations 1 or 1a, depending on whether the instrument is fixed-rate or floating-rate.

TRANSFER PRICING OF EQUITY (EQUITY CREDITING)

Funds transfer pricing methodology was introduced historically in an accrual accounting context. In traditional accounting book equity is sometimes considered "free" since the income statement does not reflect any cost of equity. It is common practice to charge an FTP rate on the complete outstanding balance of an asset. Correspondingly, an FTP credit is given on the outstanding balance of a liability. Now the assets exceed the liabilities by the amount of the book equity, which is considered free. Therefore, an equity transfer credit is given to the asset, thus reducing the overall FTP charge. In accounting sense, book equity is a fungible entity and so the equity crediting rate is typically the same for every dollar of equity, irrespective of the characteristics of the asset. The equity crediting rate is multiplied by the equity portion of the asset. The latter is determined by multiplying the book equity to asset ratio of the bank's balance sheet with the outstanding balance of the asset. The book equity to asset ratio is the same for all assets. For most financial institutions, this ratio is in the 6–10% range.

Over the years, many banks have established an economic capital framework. Along with that has emerged risk-adjusted performance measures that are more aligned to shareholder value creation. The most common of these measures is Economic Profit (see the Chapters 1 and 3 for a definition). Each transaction is attributed an economic capital reflecting all the risk in that transaction. Some banks calculate equity credit by multiplying the equity crediting rate with the economic capital attributed to the asset.

Unfortunately, this method of equity transfer crediting *overstates or understates the Economic Profit*. The calculated EP can be quite different from the true EP. In the Appendix are examples of four loans showing how the EP is overstated or understated. The magnitude of the error at the product level can be very significant, as the examples show. At the business unit level, the error may not be significant due to averaging. The magnitude of the error increases with the following: (a) the magnitude of the difference between the debt rate and the equity crediting rate, and (b) the economic capital factor.

Conceptually the correct position is to charge only the debt portion at the debt rate in so as far FTP is concerned. Then for purposes of EP calculations, charge the equity portion the cost of equity (required rate of return on equity). An alternative way of arriving at the same FTP as the above is to charge the whole outstanding balance at the debt rate and apply an equity transfer credit at the debt rate. Either of the two FTP methods leads to the same (and correct) EP. Perhaps it is easier to implement the latter instead of the former, since mechanically it is similar to the currently prevailing applications.

The examples illustrate the effect on current year EP. Even if the current EP is misstated but year to year increase/decrease in EP is not affected, then we are fine for the time being in so far as EP based *performance* and *incentive compensation* are concerned. But year to year increase/decrease in EP does get affected as significant changes in interest rates take place. The debt rate changes with changes in interest rate while the equity crediting rate is much more sluggish as it is a moving average. As a result, the overstatement/understatement in the next year can be very different from the overstatement/understatement of EP in the current year. The year to year change in EP is, therefore, also misstated.

The equity crediting methodology based on economic capital ends up with *lower transfer charge for assets with higher credit risk, everything else (including interest rate risk) being equal*. There is nothing wrong with this per se, since a higher economic capital (since equity costs more than debt) will more than make it up in a higher charge for equity. But in the initial years of introduction of economic capital, many an *incentive compensation* contract is written based on contribution margin or net revenue. Contribution margin does not include charge for equity. Consider a mezzanine loan and an investment grade senior loan (both unsecured) with identical term and amortisation schedule. The mezzanine loan attracts a 20% economic capital factor versus, say, a 5% economic capital factor for the investment grade senior loan. The former would have (significantly) higher net revenue simply because it gets a much higher equity credit. There are anecdotes of banks where at the time an economic capital framework was introduced, the business units would crave for higher economic capital since that would increase the equity crediting in the FTP mechanism and increase the contribution margin. They were being paid according to contribution margin since risk-adjusted measures had not yet been introduced in performance measurement and incentive compensation.

PREPAYMENTS AND FUNDS TRANSFER PRICING

Both assets and liabilities may have prepayment provisions usually with the option resting with the bank's customers. The most common case of prepayment is mortgage prepayments. In case of mortgages, prepayment is interest rate dependent. In case of many other products, the prepayment rate may not depend on interest rates. Many a full-blown prepayment model has been developed for pricing of mortgage-backed securities and other mortgage related products. Mortgages are very long maturity products and the principal outstanding in a pool of mortgages depends on the pool prepayment rate, which in turn depends primarily on interest rates in the future but also on other factors. But the behaviour of the principal cash flows of an individual mortgage is far less predictable. Consistent with the prevalent practice of treating mortgages as part of a pool and doing an analysis of the pool, the FTP charge on a mortgage (as part of a pool) is given by $f_\tau + OAS_\tau$, where OAS_τ is the option adjusted spread calculated from the market price prevalent at τ. The details of the computation of OAS are beyond the scope of this chapter. The reader is referred to Fabozzi (2001). Each and every mortgage in the pool is charged the FTP rate of $f_\tau + OAS_\tau$ even though some may prepay and do not have to be subject to FTP thereafter and some may not prepay at all. Since each mortgage is a small part of the portfolio, and it is near impossible to predict which particular mortgage in the pool will prepay, the application of uniform FTP rate to all mortgages, ex-ante, is justified.

In the case of a portfolio of commercial loans, however, there may be some loans which are very large in notional and whether one or more of these loans prepay has a quantum effect on the (theoretical) match funding. The timing of prepayment on a commercial loan is often random and may not be correlated with interest rates at all. It is, therefore, unfair to charge all loans an ex-ante FTP change over and above f_τ. In such a situation it is preferred to calculate a *break funding* charge at the time a particular loan pre-pays. The break funding charge is computed by taking the difference between the total of the remaining FTP charges and the (hypothetical) total of the FTP charges if the remaining balance were to be funded at the prevailing market rates at the point in which prepayment occurs.

SPREAD ON DISCOUNT RATE METHOD OF CALCULATING FTP

The two sections on FTP Rate Calculation have provided the formulae for calculating the FTP rate for an asset or a liability based on the cost of funds and principal cash flow amortisation. The methods presented equates cash flows ignoring the time value of money. Most financial institutions compute the FTP rate using either of the two sets of formulae given in the FTP Rate Calculation sections. Recently, another concept has been introduced in the calculation of FTP rate. This can be termed as spread on discount rate method. In the general form of this method, the FTP rate is a single spread, that when added to the discount rates (short rates from a term structure model), reduces the present value to the face value. This concept is similar to the concept of option-adjusted spread (OAS) in mortgages. The chapter has already introduced the prevalent FTP methodology of adding an OAS to the FTP rate f_τ in the case of a pool of mortgages in the last section. While the OAS may be calculated using a spread on discount rate, the much larger component, f_τ is still calculated using the standard method. This section introduces the spread on discount method for calculating the complete FTP rate for all products (not just mortgages).

EMBEDDED OPTIONS AND FUNDS TRANSFER PRICING

Indeterminate deposits and credit cards constitute large parts of liabilities and assets of a financial institution and have serious embedded options in favour of the customer. A particular account can increase and decrease in balance almost daily at the will of the customer. Therefore, it makes sense to calculate and apply FTP (credit or charge) to the total balance of all accounts within a particular product category rather than to an individual account. All balances in accounts within a particular product category are treated as part of "fungible dollars" moving in and out of individual accounts. Second, the principal cash flows of such "fungible dollars" have to be modelled (with strong dependence on assumptions) since there is no contractual amortisation or term. This methodology of FTP is thus fundamentally different from FTP for products with specified amortisation, even if subject to prepayment. In Chapter 8, a detailed description of this methodology has been provided.

CONCLUSION

FTP is a methodology that is essential in commercial and retail banks to determine the relative contributions of those engaged in gathering deposits and those engaged in lending money and to isolate business units in a bank from (future) fluctuations in interest rates. Treasury charges a FTP charge for each transaction on the asset side of the balance sheet and credits a FTP credit to each transaction on the liability side. The interest rate risk is computed and managed at the corporate level, generally by the Treasury function.

Our treatment of modern FTP methodology utilises the concept of opportunity cost of use of funds, which is objectively determined from the market-observed interest rate yield curves. All assets and liabilities originated at a point in time, called vintage, face the same market-observed cost of funds as the starting point. The actual FTP rate also depends on the amortisation of principal of the asset or liability. It can be calculated using a weighted average life concept or more accurately by taking all principal cash flows into account. Instruments with prepayments and with embedded options require further complexity in computation of FTP.

Transfer pricing of equity or equity crediting is not very well understood in practice in spite of its long use in financial institutions. A theoretically sound equity crediting methodology is provided keeping in mind the objective of risk-adjusted pricing and performance measures that are aligned to shareholder value creation. In the case of most retail and commercial banks, FTP is just as important a factor in risk-adjusted pricing and performance measurement as economic capital.

APPENDIX

Table A1

		Loan charactersitics		
	Loan # 1	Loan # 2	Loan # 3	Loan # 4
Vintage	mm1/yyyy1	mm2/yyyy2	mm3/yyyy3	mm4/yyyy4
Fixed/floating	Fixed	Fixed	Fixed	Floating
Amortisation schedule	Bullet	Bullet	Bullet	Bullet
Term	10 years	7 years	3 years	5 years
Outstanding (US$)	1,000,000	1,000,000	1,000,000	1,000,000
Coupon	12.50%	14.50%	9.00%	Libor + 315 bps
COF (FTP) rate	8.00%	7.75%	5.00%	Libor + 30 bps (LP)
Equity crediting rate (%)	6.25	6.25	7.25	7.25
Econ. capital factor (%)	12.00	20.00	8.00	7.00
Expected loss (%)	0.80	1.20	2.00	1.00
Non-interest expense (%)	1.00	1.50	1.00	1.00
Tax rate (%)	35.00	35.00	35.00	35.00
Reqd return on equity (%)	11.00	11.00	11.00	11.00
Libor = 6.50%				

Table A2

	Loan # 1	Loan # 2	Loan # 3	Loan # 4
Coupon cash flow (US$)	125,000	145,000	90,000	31,500
FTP charge (US$)	−80,000	−77,500	−50,000	−3,000
Equity credit (US$)	7,500	12,500	5,800	5,075
Net FTP charge (US$)	−72,500	−65,000	−44,200	2,075
Net interest margin (US$)	**52,500**	**80,000**	**45,800**	**33,575**
Non-interest expense (US$)	−10,000	−15,000	−10,000	−10,000
Expected loss (US$)	−8,000	−12,000	−20,000	−10,000
Pre-tax income (US$)	34,500	53,000	15,800	13,575
After-tax income (US$)	22,425	34,450	10,270	8,824
Charge for capital (US$)	−13,200	−22,000	−8,800	−7,700
Calculated EP (US$)	**9,225**	**12,450**	**1,470**	**1,124**
True EP (US$)	**10,590**	**14,400**	**300**	**−2,039**
Difference (%)	**Understated by 12.89**	**Understated by 13.54**	**Overstated by 390.00**	**Overstated by −155.13**
Calculated RAROC (%)	**18.69**	**17.23**	**12.84**	**12.61**
True RAROC (%)	**19.83**	**18.20**	**11.38**	**8.09**

REFERENCES

Bessis, J., 2002, *Risk Management in Banking* (Chichester: John Wiley and Sons).

Fabozzi, F. J. (ed.), 2001, *The Handbook of Mortgage-Backed Securities*, Fifth Edition (New York: McGraw Hill).

Fabozzi , F. J. (ed.), 2002, *Interest Rate, Term Structure and Valuation Modeling* (New Jersey: John Wiley & Sons).

Kafafian, R. E., 2001, "Keys to Community Bank Success: Utilizing Management Information to Make Informed Decisions – Funds Transfer Pricing, *The Journal of Bank Cost and Management Accounting*, January.

3

The Fundamentals of Economic Capital

INTRODUCTION

Economic capital is a relatively new concept. Although some of its roots can be traced to the 1980s, economic capital was introduced in financial institutions in the 1990s and has evolved into significant practical importance only in the last decade or so. A precise definition will be attempted later in the chapter. As an introduction, economic capital is a dollar number that serves as a common measure across all types of financial risks and captures the risk of unexpected losses or unexpected reductions in income in a business, a portfolio or a single transaction. Economic capital is necessarily calculated at a portfolio level and attributed to each transaction within the portfolio.

Capital investments in an industrial organisation are on physical plant, machinery and equipment. Therefore, it is relatively easy to assign specific capital investments to particular project or business unit within the corporation. As a result, deriving the capital associated with a project is very tractable. All the focus then falls on deriving the appropriate discount rate for NPV calculation. By contrast, in a financial institution, there is little physical capital investment. Deriving the capital associated with a product or a business unit within the corporation is not trivial. It needs to be explicitly derived by taking stock of the complex risks in the financial instruments associated with the business unit. Financial instruments have complex, uncertain cash flows. Elaborate analytical methodology is required to capture such risks. Risk is best captured in the computation of capital attributable to a product or business unit rather than in the discount rate. This is the genesis of economic capital and the rationale why such a concept is needed for financial institutions. This methodology is also a departure from traditional corporate finance, where the risk of cash flows from a project is reflected in the discount rate.

The need for a concept like economic capital has arisen more from practical than theoretical considerations, as financial institutions have tried to address business unit performance at levels below the corporate level performance, price products with adequate compensation for all risk, align business unit managers' objectives to shareholder value maximisation and take part in active credit portfolio management. The purpose of this chapter is to address each of these applications to illustrate why economic capital is a necessary tool for financial institutions. In what follows, the next section is a chronology, the following two sections deal with conceptual issues in economic capital, the sixth to tenth sections deal with relatively recent applications for which economic capital has become an essential tool in financial institutions, while the final section concludes the chapter.

BOOK EQUITY, REGULATORY CAPITAL AND ECONOMIC CAPITAL

From the financing side of a bank, the liability instruments are fairly identifiable. The retail core funding consists of certificate of deposit (term), indeterminate deposits with coupons ranging from wholly market-indexed to essentially administered coupons. The wholesale non-core funding consists of senior debt and subordinate debt, while the rest of wholesale financing is in the shape of trust-preferred issuance, preferred stock and common stock. In the balance sheet, the last two together constitute book equity. From another perspective, book equity can be categorised as tangible and intangible equity, which is of particular interest to rating agencies.

Until the second half of the 1990s, the amount of book equity of most financial institutions was determined by corporate finance considerations only. Attention to reported numbers like preferred target returns on book equity, tangible equity to tangible asset ratio and strategies like potential acquisition and signalling effects of share repurchase were the drivers of how much book equity must be kept (except if book capital fell below regulatory capital). It had no direct relationship to the characteristics (risk profile, term, etc) of the institution's portfolio. The question of how much capital a bank really needs, given its particular risk profile, could not be answered, even if someone asked. It was the quest for answering this important question that the need for the concept of economic capital was first felt (see Parsley, 1995).

From the risk measurement side of the bank, economic capital is for the unexpected losses or unexpected reduction in income. For a long tailed (say, loss) distribution, extreme events can be associated with significant probability density. The less diversified the portfolio the fatter the tail. These events, although not catastrophic, can cause huge losses for a bank in one year with extremely good performance for many years previous to the bad year. So much so that loss in one or two portfolios can wipe out the entire positive income from the rest of the bank, with depletion of accumulated reserves to boot.[1] Occurrence of such events in some banks in the late 1980s and early 1990s prompted significant interest in understanding tail risk and portfolio diversification in the wholesale credit world. This also prompted the development of the analytical framework from which economic capital evolved.

Financial institutions (banks and insurance companies in particular) are highly regulated with minimum regulatory capital requirements. Therefore, to the extent that it becomes binding, regulatory capital becomes a constraint. Regulatory capital is based on simplistic formulations and has little correspondence with risk of the portfolios of a bank. This is likely to change with the impending Basel II[2] Accord, which seeks to align regulatory capital to risk more closely than in the present capital accord. Basel II is to take effect in January 2008 and regulatory capital and internal economic capital are in a path of convergence. Until such time, regulated financial institutions will have to deliberate on the comparison and reconcilement of internally calculated economic capital with regulatory capital requirements. Given the one-size-fits-all nature of the present accord, the exercise is best done at the corporation level, with product pricing exclusively driven by internal economic capital.

DEPARTURE FROM STANDARD CORPORATE FINANCE

In corporate finance the risk of investments in different projects is traditionally captured by applying different discount rates to the stream of cash flows from those projects. The discount rate is meant to measure uncertainty in cash flows associated with different projects – the higher the uncertainty, the higher the discount rate. Stated differently, the cost of capital for each project is different depending on the uncertainty of cash flows generated by each project. Also in standard corporate finance, the financing decision can be separated from the investing decision. This implies that the discount rate or cost of capital associated with each project with differing levels of cash flow uncertainty cannot be derived from the observed cost of capital from the financing function of the corporation as a whole.

It is a daunting task to calculate the appropriate discount rate (actual rate per cent, not rank ordering) for different projects in an industrial company (see Brealy and Myers, 1996) for a conceptual treatment of the issues involved). The task becomes more difficult when the company is a conglomerate with activities in diverse industries because the risks are so different. It is perhaps even more difficult for a financial institution (though all its activities are in one industry) because the risks in financial instruments are complex and cover a whole spectrum. In this context, it may be useful to state the ways in which a financial institution differs from an industrial organisation – differences that are particularly relevant in establishing the need for the concept of economic capital for financial institutions.

Unlike most industrial organisations, capital investment for a financial institution is not on tangible plant, machinery and equipment. The physical assets of a financial institution are a small fraction of its total assets, which consist mostly of financial assets (even for a "bricks and mortar" retail bank). The risk of a bank's primarily financial assets comes from the uncertainty of the complex and often contingent, stream of cash flows associated with the financial assets. The broad categories of risks that need to be quantified are credit risk, market risk, prepayment risk, liquidity risk, insurance risk, operational risk and business or strategic risk.[3] The spectrum of risk within each category can be very wide and not easily comparable without a technically sound methodology.

Banks are highly leveraged, with debt to equity ratios in excess of fifteen-to-one, in comparison with industrial firms. Most of the debt liabilities are in the shape of customer deposits, which are insured by the federal government under the deposit insurance programme. This is one reason perceived market risk of a bank stock is much less than the debt to equity ratio may imply, everything else being equal. Relatively speaking, a bank is in a position to raise capital rather cheaply. This is less true of other forms of financial institutions.

In an industrial organisation the capital investments are on physical plant, machinery and equipment. It is relatively easy to identify which of the capital investments relate to which project or business unit within the corporation. Therefore, deriving the capital associated with a project is very tractable. All the focus then falls on deriving the appropriate discount rate for NPV calculation. In a financial institution, there is little physical capital investment. Deriving the capital associated with a product or a business unit within the corporation is not trivial. It needs to be explicitly derived by taking stock of the complex risks in the financial instruments associated with the business unit.

In recent years, this departure from standard corporate finance approach, taken by financial institutions and consulting firms while introducing the concept of economic capital, has been applied in the context of non-financial companies as well (see Stein *et al*, 2002 and Tierny and Smithson, 2003).

A SINGLE COST PER UNIT OF ECONOMIC CAPITAL
If all the risks in different portfolios of financial instruments are captured in the measure of economic capital needed to support the portfolios, then it makes sense to assign all the portfolios identical cost per unit of economic capital. The corporate cost of equity or the required rate of return on equity that investors require is much easier to determine from market observations in the financing side. This is a single number or rate irrespective of the business unit, portfolio or transaction. The problem of finding the appropriate discount rate for different levels of risk is thus shifted to the problem of finding the appropriate economic capital. As it turns out, the problem of finding the appropriate economic capital is complex but can be approached from analytically sound (reasonably) principles using observed price and default data. The same cannot be said of the problem of arriving at an appropriate discount rate.

The most common way of determining the required rate of return for a company's stock is to use the capital asset pricing model (CAPM), which has been prevalent in the finance literature for decades. The following CAPM formula gives the expected or required rate of return, k, for the company's common stock as follows:

$$k = r_f + \beta \cdot [E(r_m) - r_f] \tag{1}$$

where r_f is the return on a risk-free asset, β is the beta of the stock – a measure of its systematic risk and $E(r_m)$ is the expected return on the market (say S&P 500 index). The term in the [...] is referred to as the market risk premium. For most US banks, the cost of equity capital calculated using the above formula is between 10% and 15%. The exact rate depends not only on long-term historical observations but also on the current rate environment.

The use of CAPM for calculating the cost of equity capital is analytically simple but is not straightforward when it comes to implementation. Judgement is called for in the estimation of all the three elements: market risk premium, risk-free rate and the institution's beta (see Pettit, 1999, for a detailed exposition of the implementation issues). Clearly, the estimated cost of equity number can be different depending on the exact methodology and length of historical data used by the bank. But, once arrived at, the cost of equity is not likely to be a major (and on-going) management debate in a financial institution. In fact, a single cost of equity capital for all businesses and all products is a boon since all business units are treated equally in this regard.

A PRECISE DEFINITION OF ECONOMIC CAPITAL AND ITS PRACTICAL DIFFICULTIES

The most widely used definition of economic capital is the following: *the potential unexpected (dollar) loss of economic value over one year calculated at a pre-specified confidence level*. The level of confidence is anchored by the desired insolvency standard of the financial institution. Given the desired bond rating of the institution, a probability of insolvency over one year can be determined from historical bond default data. The confidence level is one minus the probability of insolvency. This is sometimes referred to as the debt-holders' perspective (see Hall, 2002).

The definition of economic capital (EC) has similar elements as the definition of the more familiar value-at-risk (VAR), commonly used in the market risk world. But it is pertinent to mention the differences.

❑ First, conceptually the horizon in trading VAR calculation is the period that is necessary to unwind a position. One day is the most common horizon used for VAR. Conceptually, the horizon in EC calculation is the period over which an institution can rebuild its capital or restructure its capital financing. One year is the horizon that has come to be in common use.

❑ Second, the level of confidence (usually 95%) used in trading VAR calculation is much lower in comparison with the level of confidence used in EC calculation. Most financial institutions have a debt rating of Triple B to Double A. The corresponding insolvency standard requires the specification of a very high confidence level ranging from 99.5% to 99.97%. Third, VAR is associated with market risk oversight only. EC has come to play a role in many aspects of a financial institution from pricing to incentive compensation.

❑ In common parlance, a 95% confidence level means that the portfolio value can be expected to go down by the daily VAR (calculated ex-ante) once every 20 business days or so. A trader or manager used to profit and loss volatility can grasp this easily. She or he expects to see an event reaching the VAR limit once in a while and several times during her/his tenure. At 99.9% confidence level, EC is to cover annual losses in all years except once in 1,000 years. When a manager thinks about this, she or he can come to the conclusion that such a rare event may not occur in her or his whole career. The natural inference is that the business unit is being allocated too much economic capital. By that logic, so is every other business unit.

Another way of defining economic capital is more empirical. This is to start from volatility of income or net operating profit after taxes (NOPAT). In corporate finance, risk arises precisely from volatility of cash flows. If a financial institution had reliable historical data and assuming the future will follow the pattern of the past, then the volatility or standard deviation of income can be estimated. Economic capital is then a suitable multiplier of the volatility.

Alternatively an empirical distribution can be fitted to the data and we can go from there.

Unfortunately reliable historical data over a sufficiently long period is rarely available at the corporation level, let alone at the business unit level. Moreover many financial institutions change their business mix (and consequently risk profile) significantly as a result of mergers and acquisitions from time to time.

A structural model of economic capital requires estimation of parameters, which can be done using market information or industry pooled information and then the loss or value distribution is generated by the model either by analytical means or by Monte Carlo simulation. If an analytically sound structural model is available for the risk in question, it is preferred to a purely empirical model for economic capital. A pragmatic economic capital methodology for a diversified financial institution is to utilise the structural model path for all risks (eg, credit risk or market risk) that can be captured by such models and then fall back on the volatility of income approach for those risks for which structural models do not exist (eg, fiduciary risk or risk from a brokerage business).

SHAREHOLDER VALUE CREATION

A simple definition of shareholder return for a company is the sum of the dividend yield and the relative price appreciation of the common stock of the company over a specified period. The excess shareholder return by the company over that period is the difference between the shareholder return and the required rate of return. The latter has already been introduced on p 38. Shareholder value is created as a result of this excess return. However, this simple statement needs to be paraphrased.

First, on the basis of price-earnings ratio, the market seems to reward those companies that have a high excess shareholder return and a high growth of revenue. Thus, while having top-line growth alone is not enough, shrinking revenue by divestiture in order to increase excess shareholder return is not a good idea either. Until recently financial institutions have focused most of their attention to top-line growth, with measures like return on assets (ROA) and contribution margin as drivers of performance.

Second, much more attention is paid by a financial institution as to how it has performed relative to peers (or to some benchmark) than to shareholder value created by the organisation. This diverts attention to comparisons on several reported measures (some of which are cosmetic rather than economic) instead of attention to shareholder value creation.

Third, it is likely that there are business units within the financial institution, which contribute negatively to shareholder value creation. Within a limited period of time, it is perfectly legitimate to continue with those business units as long as they reduce the magnitude of their negative contribution (ie, show improvement over time, even though negative) – particularly, if they add significantly to revenue growth.

Finally, the stock price is affected by many factors on which neither the corporate manager nor the business unit manager has any influence. Therefore, particularly for the business units, it is necessary to have a measure that is, by and large, directly influenced by the business unit managers and at the same time is strongly correlated with shareholder value creation. Stern Stewart's EVA (economic value added) is one such measure. It has been shown that EVA has by far the strongest correlation with market value creation than any other profitability measure like earnings per share (EPS), net income (NI), return on book equity (ROE) or return on assets (ROA). This is true for financial companies as well as industrial companies (see Uyemura, 1997; Uyemura *et al*, 1996 for details).

The shareholder value creation imperative has received attention in financial institutions somewhat later than it did in many industrial organisations. Banks have introduced performance measures similar to EVA such as shareholder value added (SVA), economic profit (EP) or economic profit added (EPA) with a view to enhance shareholder value creation. Other banks have introduced ratio measures such as return on risk adjusted capital (RORAC) or risk-adjusted return on capital (RAROC).

Single-period economic profit will be defined as simply:

$$EP = NI - k \cdot EC \tag{2}$$

where NI is net income, k is the required return on equity and EC is economic capital. This is a risk adjusted measure. The value of the measure is not as much in corporate performance as in business unit performance measurement. It must be obvious to the reader that without a methodology to calculate economic capital capturing all forms of risk in financial instruments it is not possible to calculate EP at various levels of a financial institution. Thus the shareholder value creation imperative in financial institutions needed the concept of economic capital to precede it. The shift in paradigm from traditional measures to EP or RORAC is intimately tied to the introduction of economic capital.

The EP formula is for ex-post measurement. The ex-ante measure simply replaces NI by expected NI. The ratio measure, single-period return on risk adjusted capital is defined as:

$$RORAC = NI/EC \qquad (3)$$

Notice that in the above formula, the adjustment for risk has been captured in the denominator (risk-adjusted capital) and not in the numerator. The numerator does have provision for expected losses that may arise particularly from credit risk. But expected losses are considered part of doing a credit business rather than a risk. Also RORAC is greater than k if EP is positive and vice-versa.

Economic profit is derived from accounting results easily available in a financial institution's general ledger, except for economic capital. Economic capital is, therefore, the only unfamiliar driver of economic profit. As a result, in the implementation of a new performance system aimed at shareholder value creation, most of the attention falls on economic capital.

With the establishment of a comprehensive economic capital framework, economic profit can be computed not only for the corporation but also for business units and further down. Economic profit is additive and can be cumulated from one level to the next. Each business unit manager can see the direct connection between his or her actions and performance and that unit's economic profit, by and large independent of the performance of other business units. These three properties are not possessed by share price or market value of equity. There is only one share price for the corporation. It is impossible to derive a variable at the business unit level that can add up to the market value of equity. The share price is affected by the performance of all the businesses together as well as exogenous factors beyond the control of the business unit managers. Hence the value of economic profit as a performance measure is more at the business unit level than at the corporation level. It helps when cascading the shareholder value creation paradigm down through the organisation.

Economic capital has provided the means for financial institutions to devise a performance measure that leads to shareholder value maximisation. But that is not enough. Leading institutions have also tied compensation to economic profit. Such a compensation system has economic profit as the primary driver, coupled with several other qualitative performance indicators. This helps further aligning managers' objectives to shareholder value creation.

PRICING FOR RISK AND PRODUCT PROFITABILITY
Of all the applications of economic capital in a financial institution, pricing every product appropriately to ensure that the institution is getting adequate return for the risk taken is perhaps the most important. A pricing model calculates a break-even price, incorporating accurate funding cost, all-in expense (overhead as well as direct), expected loss provisions and economic capital.

Pricing of traditional bank products have often been subjective in the past, based on imperfect knowledge of competitors' prices in the geographic region and making a choice to target somewhere in the range of competitors' prices. To this day, many a bank's pricing of retail deposits follows this subjective pattern, except in geographies where the bank is by far the dominant player. In credit products, however, pricing has long taken provision for expected loss into account. What has been lacking is taking into account the economic capital that is needed to cover unexpected losses. It is appropriate to enumerate here the distinction between expected loss and unexpected loss:

❏ Expected loss (EL) is the mean value of all possible losses the transaction or the portfolio can experience over one year. Expected loss of a portfolio is the sum of the expected loss of each transaction in the portfolio. Expected loss depends only on the risk characteristics of the transactions. The primary drivers of credit risk in a transaction are many eg, financial ratios of the obligor (the company to which the credit has been advanced by the financial institution), collateral, guarantees, size of open credit line etc. But they all collapse to determine three commonly used parameters namely, probability of obligor default (PD), loss in the event of default (LIED) or loss given default (LGD) and exposure at default (EAD). The first two are usually expressed as percentages and the last one is obviously a dollar number.

$$EL\ (\$) = EAD \cdot PD \cdot LGD \qquad\qquad (4)$$

$$EL\ (\%) = PD \cdot LGD \qquad\qquad (4a)$$

❏ Unexpected loss of a portfolio cannot be obtained by summing unexpected losses, however determined, of each transaction. Unexpected loss of a portfolio depends on all the risk characteristics mentioned above of all the transactions in the portfolio. But it also depends upon a very important portfolio characteristic – portfolio correlation. When the economy (or a particular sector of the economy) goes bad, not all obligors' fates go together. Default of one obligor does not necessarily mean another one in the portfolio will default at the same time. The portfolio correlation is less than unity. The more diversified the portfolio, the less is the correlation. The lower the correlation, the less is the unexpected loss of a portfolio. Correlation is at the root of the sometimes counter-intuitive result that a portfolio with seemingly riskier individual assets (higher EL) than another could still have a low EC because of diversification. For example a granular portfolio of diversified (across different industries and geographies) middle market loans may have an EL of 1.2% while a commercial real estate (CRE) portfolio consisting of a limited number of large projects concentrated in certain geographies may have an EL of 0.9%. Yet the EC required to support the middle market portfolio may be less than the EC required to support the CRE portfolio.

Economic capital, as defined on p 38 of this chapter, is the potential unexpected (dollar) loss over one year calculated at a pre-specified confidence level.

$$EC = EAD \cdot G(PD, LGD, Correlations) \qquad\qquad (5)$$

where $G(\ldots)$ is a complex function. Notice that generally, EC is not a direct one-to-one function of EL.

Figure 1 illustrates the concepts of expected loss, unexpected loss and economic capital for credit risk in a portfolio.

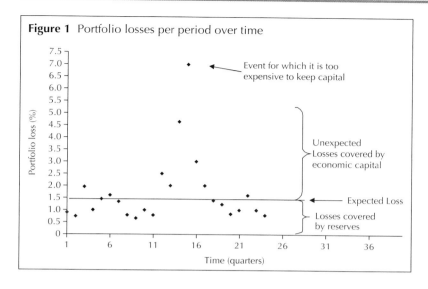

Figure 1 Portfolio losses per period over time

The number and values of the data points are for illustrative purposes only. Computing portfolio economic capital at a very high confidence level empirically is almost impossible, since the amount of consistent historical data necessary is rarely available. The function $G(\ldots)$ is derived from a structural model instead.

More sophisticated models may capture the interrelationship between default and LGD since recoveries are likely to be lower in bad economic times, when defaults are higher. Notice that $LGD = 1 -$ Recovery. Also LGD in Equation 5 is really expected LGD. A distribution of LGD may be captured in sophisticated models. The functional form $G(\ldots)$ in Equation 5 becomes more and more complex. The correlation in Equation 5 is intra-portfolio correlation. In addition, inter-portfolio correlations (eg, across different industries or geographies, between retail portfolio and wholesale portfolio) may be incorporated in sophisticated economic capital models.

Product pricing essentially consist of setting fees and coupons in such a way that the RORAC calculated over the life of the product exceeds a break-even rate. The break-even rate can be set at some value equal to or higher than the required return on equity, k. Equivalently, the economic profit present valued over the life of the product exceeds a break-even value. The break-even EP can be set at some value equal to or higher than zero. Typically a pricing model allows the user to select reasonable fee and coupon rate combinations that the market is likely to bear and also breaks even. Any combination of fee and coupon over and above that ensures that the product is profitable to the financial institution in the sense of adding to shareholder value. Economic capital is a major driver of the results of a pricing model but is by no means the only major driver.

CUSTOMER PROFITABILITY

Financial institutions have long been interested in the profitability of an overall relationship or of a customer as a whole and on retaining the best customers. Billions of dollars have been spent by financial institutions in the USA on customer relationship management systems, which go well beyond profitability. Generally, such investments have not yielded the desired return on investment, for various reasons. One of the less important ones is that customer profitability measures are not fully risk adjusted. In a highly competitive (pricing) environment, this is a fatal deficiency, at least in the long run.

A commercial or retail customer typically has many different products offered by a financial institution. These products range from loans to deposits to services for a fee. From the perspective of the financial institution, some of these products have credit risk, some have prepayment risk, some have operational risk, some have fiduciary risk, and so on and so forth. In this respect, risk of a relationship is far more complex than the risk of a single product, which is much more tractable.

For customer profitability, therefore, economic capital as a common measure of risk across such disparate products is essential. It is easy to add or subtract revenues and expenses (and even loan loss reserves) across all such products in a relationship and come up with the traditional customer profitability measure common today. But it is much more difficult to derive measures like contribution to shareholder value or return on equity for customer profitability, without a well-established economic capital framework for all important products of the financial institution. In a highly competitive environment, it is likely that a large chunk of customers may appear marginally profitable under the current customer profitability measures while they may actually erode shareholder value.

A MULTI-PERIOD PERSPECTIVE

In dealing with traditional loan and deposit products, the cash flows are primarily coupon payments and principal payments. These payments may occur over several years. For such margin income products, a multi-period perspective and a single-period perspective generate similar results in terms of performance measures. But in recent years, financial institutions have progressively enhanced their income coming from fees (which are typically one-time rather than recurring cash flows) compared with margin income. The existence of such one-time cash flows in significant proportions makes it imperative to take a multi-period view.

Economic capital has been defined to cover risk of unexpected events occurring over one year. How, then, does it reconcile with the multi-period view? It is incorrect to think that recourse to marked-to-market (as against default only) economic capital, for transactions with terms in excess of one year, takes care of it. Marked-to-market economic capital covers losses due to possible migration as well as losses due to default. However, the horizon is still one year.

The multi-period profitability measures can be derived as follows:

$$EP(multi\text{-}period) = PV(NI) - k \cdot PV(EC) \qquad (6)$$

$$RORAC(multi\text{-}period) = \frac{PV(NI)}{PV(EC)} \qquad (7)$$

where PV is present value calculated using k as the discount rate. The relationship, that $RORAC$ is greater than k if EP is positive, holds only if the discount rate k is used and not some other rate of discount.

Pricing based on economic capital is an ex-ante exercise. It must take into account the effects of a single transaction or vintage over multiple periods (say, years). The multi-period EP may be positive for a product (with significant one time cash flows) but in one or more of the periods the EP contribution may be negative. Performance measurement based on shareholder value creation, on the other hand, is an ex-post exercise. Typically such performance is of a single manager or a business unit and takes into account the effects, in the period (quarter or year in question), of numerous transactions across several vintages.

It is important to clearly understand the above distinctions between pricing and performance measurement and their ramifications. In the absence of such understanding, discrepancies in measured results will invariably be blamed on the economic capital methodology. In truth, the economic capital methodology is usually consistent across both applications. The numbers from the pricing and performance measurement will rarely be the same and there are logical reasons why they differ in many cases. In credit products the difference is particularly significant at the bottom or top of the economic cycle.

ACTIVE CREDIT PORTFOLIO MANAGEMENT AND ECONOMIC CAPITAL

The loan portfolios of many commercial and retail banks consist of borrowers whose names do not trade publicly. The customers underlying a retail portfolio may have bureau scores available but there is no active market for trading of such portfolios, just as there is no active market for trading of loans to private firms. That is not to say that there is no active securitisation market, eg, of mortgages or credit cards or other retail assets. But most financial institutions view the securitisation market as a source of funding rather than from the perspective of active credit[4] portfolio management.

In recent years active credit portfolio management has become a discipline for financial institutions to go from a buy-and-hold mode to a mode of active repositioning of their overall portfolio credit risk, especially with the development of the credit default swap market. However, a liquid credit default swap market exists only for highly rated names and there is market for private names. Active credit portfolio management is, therefore, mostly restricted to the institutional portfolio consisting of corporates with public ratings and publicly traded stocks. Another offshoot of active credit portfolio management in large financial institutions is the arms-length separation that is possible between originators on the one hand and portfolio managers on the other. For each name in the institutional portfolio, the observed or implied spreads in the capital markets (bond market, credit default swap market or collateralised debt obligation market) can be used to "transfer price" the transaction moving from the originator to the portfolio manager.

Financial institutions with assets, for which there is no direct or implied spread observed in the capital markets, cannot easily take part in such active credit portfolio management. A well-developed economic capital framework (in this instance economic capital for credit risk) with explicit intra and inter portfolio correlations can enable a financial institution to fruitfully participate in active credit portfolio management and, through a mapping, to transfer price credit transactions. The details of such an application are contained in Chapter 7.

CONCLUSION

The applications discussed in the previous sections demonstrate the significance of the concept of economic capital. Since financial institutions differ from industrial organisations in terms of their focus on financial assets and the associated uncertainty and complexity of cash flows, there is a need for a concept such as economic capital to serve as a tool for analysis and assessment of risk, pricing, credit management, shareholder value maximisation and measurement of performance both at the corporate and business unit level.

As the applications demonstrate, economic capital adequately captures unexpected losses or reduction in income and is useful for analysing portfolio diversification in wholesale credit. The concept of economic capital is also particularly relevant for financial institutions in view of the Basel II accord, which seeks to align regulatory capital requirements in accord with portfolio risk for banks. The spectrum of risk associated with financial assets is wide and requires a sound methodology to assess and quantify risk. The concept of economic capital provides a unified method of measuring risk within and across portfolios and business units. There are both empirical and structural models of economic capital, which may be used for risk assessment by financial institutions. Another significant use of economic capital is in measuring shareholder value creation. Financial institutions need the concept of economic capital for performance measurement through tools such as risk-adjusted returns on capital. The concept of economic capital enables performance measurement at both the unit level and at the corporate level and aligns business decisions closely with profitability in contrast with traditional measures such as the share price which is influenced by exogenous factors and fails to measure each unit's contribution to the organisation's goals.

The contribution of economic capital to pricing of products in financial institutions and for assessing customer profitability similarly rest on its ability to assess and measure risks and uncertainties within a consistent framework. The economic capital framework lends itself well to a multi-period perspective and is effective for both pricing and performance measurement. The concept of economic capital enables large financial institutions in active credit portfolio management through effective transfer pricing of securities as they move from originators to portfolio managers.

1 This is not to say that the accumulated equity capital is wiped out – far from it!
2 See introduction (pp 1 to 5) in Basel Committee on Banking Supervision (2003)
3 For an exhaustive list and description of types of financial risk, see Porteous *et al* (2003)
4 In fact, a good understanding of the credit risk in securitisation tranches has come about only in the last few years (see Gordy and Jones, 2003; Pykhtin and Dev, 2002, 2003).

REFERENCES

Basel Committee on Banking Supervision, 2003, *International Convergence of capital Measurements and Capital Standards: A Revised Framework,* Bank for International Settlements, June.

Brealy, R. A. and S. C. Myers, 1996, *Principles of Corporate Finance* (New York: McGraw-Hill).

Gordy, M. and D. Jones, 2003, "Random Tranches," *Risk,* pp 78–83, March.

Hall, C., 2002, "Economic Capital: Towards an Integrated Framework", *Risk,* pp 33–6, October,

Parsley, M., 1995, The RORAC Revolution, *Euromoney,* pp 36–41, October.

Pettit, J., 1999, Corporate Capital Cost: A Practitioner's Guide, *Journal of Applied Corporate Finance,* **12(1),** pp 113–20.

Porteous, B., L. McCulloch, and P. Tapadar, 2003, An Approach to Economic Capital for Financial Services Firms, *Risk,* pp 28–31, April.

Pykhtin, M. and A. Dev, 2002, Credit Risk in Asset Securitizations: an Analytical Model, *Risk,* pp S16–S20, May.

Pykhtin, M. and A. Dev, 2003, Coarse-grained CDOs, *Risk,* pp 113–16, January.

Stein, J. C., S. E. Usher, D. LaGattuta, and J. Youngen, 2002, A Comparables Approach to Measuring Cashflow-at-Risk for Non-financial Firms, *Journal of Applied Corporate Finance,* **13(4),** pp 27–40.

Tierny, J. and C. Smithson, 2003, Implementing Economic Capital in an Industrial Company: the case of Michelin, *Journal of Applied Corporate Finance,* **15(4)**, pp 81–94.

Uyemura, D. G., 1997, EVA: A Top-Down Approach to Risk Management, *Journal of Lending and Credit Risk Management,* **79(6)**, p 40.

Uyemura, D. G., C. C. Cantor, and J. M. Pettit, 1996, EVA for banks: Value creation, risk management and profitability measurement, *Journal of Applied Corporate Finance,* **9(2)**, pp 94–113.

4

Expense Allocation

INTRODUCTION

Earlier chapters introduced the concepts of funds transfer pricing and economic capital. These are *two of the three legs* of internal performance measurement in a financial institution. The *third leg* is costing or expense assignment. The methodologies involved in both funds transfer pricing and economic capital are analytically complex and relatively new. In contrast, expense assignment is analytically less challenging and has been in existence for a long time. Yet in terms of getting one's arms around it, the third leg is perhaps the most difficult.

Financial institutions offer a number of products and services from the same branch or business unit and several business units share common systems and service in order to continue their business. Therefore, in order to assess the performance of a product or a business unit, it is necessary to be able to apportion the cost of shared location, system or service to the products that benefit from them. In today's world of application systems, data mining, analytics and multi-product offerings it is difficult to determine in advance how much to charge each product. Yet product pricing requires these inputs and ultimately determine the profitability of the product or the relationship.

Financial institutions often report a high level "expense ratio". For most financial institutions, expense ratio is over 50%. That means, expenses are over half of the revenues for the institution as a whole. A majority of such expenses are incurred on shared systems and services. The very materiality of expenses requires that a well-founded expense allocation methodology be established in order to measure performance accurately. There is another reason why this is even more important. It is easy to see from the general ledger that overall such expenses are being incurred. If the cost or expense allocation methodology is crude, all products get charged something like an "average" expense. Those that do not consume much expense will show lower profitability than actual profitability and other products will show higher profitability than is truly the case. Consistent inaccuracy and distortions in profitability measurements can lead a bank to be priced out of an essentially profitable but highly competitive business and more and more into only "apparently" profitable businesses. A third reason for the importance of a reasonable objective expense allocation mechanism is that it minimises the otherwise interminable discussions amongst numerous stakeholders about what is right and what is wrong in terms of cost allocation. Much more so than in funds transfer pricing and economic capital methodologies, everyone seems to have an opinion as to what should be the "correct" expense allocation methodology.

EXPENSE ALLOCATION IN PERFORMANCE MEASUREMENT

The concepts of fixed and variable costs are familiar ones in economics. Fixed cost does not depend on the quantity produced while variable cost is a (generally increasing) function of the quantity produced. This simple dichotomy does not quite hold in a financial institution. With the constant introduction of new and complex products and repeated mergers and acquisitions in the financial industry, even the most traditional of overheads are not strictly fixed. Nevertheless, at the minimum a broad distinction between "direct" expenses and "overhead" expenses is made by almost all financial institutions.

Let us consider performance of a fixed rate loan transaction originated at time τ for the calendar period $\tau + t$ to $\tau + t + 1$. Although monthly or quarterly period computations are common as well as yearly, here we assume for illustrative purposes, that the period is a year. Two of the most common traditional performance measures are contribution margin (CM) and net income (NI):

$$CM(t) = Revenue(t) - Cost_{debt}(t) - Exp_{direct} - Loss(t)$$

$$NI(t) = (1 - tax\_rate) * [CM - Exp_{overhead}]$$

Let us consider an illustrative but realistic[1] numerical example: Balance outstanding at $\tau + t$ on the loan: US$100,000; Coupon: 7.00%; FTP rate given the cost of funds at origination τ: 4.00%; a fee of US$200 is received and no loss incurred in the period $\tau + t$ to $\tau + t + 1$. Let $EC(t)$ for the loan be US$6,000 corresponding to a capital factor of 6.00%. The debt portion is, therefore, US$94,000. Then, $Revenue(t) = $ US$7,200 and $Cost_{debt}(t) = $ US$4,000 (=4.26% * 94,000) and $Loss(t) = 0$. Let direct expenses be 100 bps (or 1.00%) of the outstanding balance. Thus, net interest margin, $NIM(t) = 300$ bps and $CM(t) = $ US$2,200 or 220 bps of the balance. Let the allocated overhead expenses to this loan be US$1,000 and the effective tax_rate be 35%. Then, $NI(t) = (1 - 0.35) \cdot (US2,200 - US1,000) = $ US$780 which translates to a return on asset, $ROA(t) = 78$ bps.

A risk-adjusted performance measure is economic profit, $EP(t)$:

$$EP(t) = NI(t) - k * EC(t)$$

Let the required return on equity capital for the institution be $k = 14\%$. The economic profit, $EP(t)$ is negative: $-$US$60. This loan actually *erodes shareholder value* even though it creates a positive $CM(t) = $ US$2,200.

If on the other hand, the direct expenses were only 90 bps of the outstanding balance and the allocated overheads were US$900, the following would have been the performances: $CM(t) = $ US$2,300, $NI(t) = $ US$910 and $EP(t) = $ US$70. The loan now *adds to shareholder value*.

Such a major shift in performance of a loan simply by a reduction of 10 bps in expenses illustrates the *need for a fairly accurate measurement of expenses and their allocation*. Most of the direct expenses and all of the overheads are related to shared systems and services in today's financial institutions. Averaging of all direct costs associated with a portfolio of loans is inadequate. Some loans (eg, high quality large size loans) may consume less than average time and money from the shared systems and services per unit dollar outstanding. The difference can easily be 10 bps or more. As we saw in the preceding example, this makes all the difference between a loan being adjudged profitable or not, on a risk-adjusted basis.

The example above focused only on a single loan. It is easy to see that the basic point is valid for any single product. Certain kinds of products consume relatively few systems and services but they tend to be people intensive with high compensation expense. The argument can also be extended to a portfolio or a business unit as well.

APPROACHES TO EXPENSE ALLOCATION

Of the three legs of performance measurement in a financial institution, expense allocation (including the associated costing methodology) is the most labour-intensive. It is also the one which sparks the most prolonged discussions and almost everyone around the table generally has a different opinion as to what the appropriate methodology and numbers are. This is perhaps because, unlike funds transfer pricing and economic capital, it is possible to pass judgement on aspects of expense allocation without having high levels of technical expertise. In most financial institutions, the details of expense allocation methodology deployed are the culmination of many compromises among the stakeholders.

However, at a slightly higher level, the basic approaches are generally common across financial institutions. These approaches are *direct allocation, sequential allocation* and *simultaneous allocation*. Which one of the three approaches is appropriate to a financial institution depends on several characteristics of the institution, including complexity of products, extent of shared systems and services, resources devoted to costing and management accounting and the way in which the information is used. In some cases, the choice also depends on the subjective compromise that is acceptable.

The *direct allocation approach* distributes all expenses directly to the final profit centres. The expense flows are mutually exclusive. The term profit centre is used in a general sense for any unit that is responsible for generating revenue and maintaining customer relationship. Under this approach, no expense is allocated to support services, administrative services, processing, etc. These are support centres instead of profit centres. Each expense allocation flow originates as an actual direct expense of a support centre. The direct expense of a support centre flows into many profit centres as allocated (sometimes crudely referred to as "overhead") expense. But the flow may not be through a straight connection between the support centre and a profit centre, as the following example illustrates.

In a financial institution, asset management PC services (AMPCS), a support centre, provides software and hardware maintenance to fiduciary risk management, another support centre. Both provide support to asset management and investment advisory, two of the profit centres in the institution. Under direct allocations approach all expenses of the AMPCS unit are allocated to asset management and investment advisory, including the expenses associated with maintaining the PC services of fiduciary risk management. The proportions of the expense allocated to asset management and investment advisory respectively are determined by identified "cost drivers".

The advantage of the direct allocation approach lies in its simplicity. The part of the expenses of a support centre providing services to another support centre is allocated to the ultimate profit centres directly. The profit centres are not direct users of such services and there may not be a suitable cost driver to base the allocation across profit centres. The resulting allocation numbers to the profit centres lack credibility.

The *sequential allocation approach* allocates expense iteratively through a series of allocations in a pre-specified sequence. A support centre's expenses are allocated to both profit centres and support centres that utilise its services. The latter are referred to as "intermediate users". At the next iteration, the expenses of such an intermediate user are allocated to the ultimate profit centres. Once a support centre's expenses have been distributed, that centre is no longer able to receive expense allocations. At each iteration, several such centres are "closed" and the number of centres eligible to receive expense flows is considerably reduced. At the end, only the profit centres, the final beneficiaries of the services, remain with the corresponding expense allocations.

The sequential allocation approach is obviously more complex but is more accurate than the direct allocation approach. It is more difficult to track expense flows and to keep an audit trail. But the biggest drawback is that the final expense numbers allocated to profit centres depends strongly on the sequence selected. Thus starting with the same support centres and profit centres and the same expense levels pre-allocation, the computed expense allocation will be different for different allocation sequences.

Under the *simultaneous allocation approach*, expenses of a support centre are distributed to profit centres and all other support centres that utilise its services. In turn, it receives expense allocations from those support centres concurrently. Thus there are positive and negative flows to each support centre. When a support centre receives an allocation, that expense is allocated to all users of its services in a way determined by the cost drivers. To derive final allocation numbers from a simultaneous allocation approach, complex mathematical techniques have to be used, often with the help of some computer software. The two techniques used are "continuous iterations" until all the support centres are left with negligible expense and solving "simultaneous linear equations".

The advantage of the simultaneous allocation approach is the level of accuracy it can achieve. But its complexity makes it difficult to understand and perform manual calculations. The mathematical equations that are often needed to solve in a simultaneous allocation approach throws off many a banker, who then treats the expense allocation as a black-box. The computer program invariably used to implement the simultaneous allocation approach often is able to keep track of the flow of expenses and so provide an audit trail.

ACTIVITY-BASED COSTING

Activity-based costing (ABC) was first introduced in manufacturing companies, starting in the late 1980s. Since then ABC has become a costing discipline in its own right and has been extended to service industries. Financial institutions have been late adopters of ABC and it is yet to become commonplace in the financial sector.

In contrast to traditional cost accounting, ABC focuses on "processes" rather than "financial transactions" – processes are made of "activities" of work. Occasionally a single constitutuent may constitute the whole of a less complex process. From a "six-sigma" or "continuous improvement" perspective, processes are easy to understand, analyse and redesign for both cost and quality improvements.

It is impossible to do a good analysis by looking at financial transactions. Therein lies the common link between process redesign and ABC. Both have been used extensively in manufacturing organisations. In theory, ABC takes a financial institution from ad-hoc cost management to understanding the causes of costs. It also creates a common ground between financial accounting and the business units in a financial institution – business unit managers are more familiar with work processes, which they live through every day, than with accounting entries.

The causes of costs are called *cost drivers*. In ABC, cost drivers must be quantifiable. There are usually two levels of drivers: *resource drivers* and *activity drivers*. A *cost object* is a product, relationship, business unit, marketing initiative or any other unit which an ABC cost measurement is done. Cost objects can be thought of as "to what and for whom work is done" (quote from Smith and Harper, 2001, which the reader may refer to for a more detailed implementation of ABC in banks). Resource drivers map expenditures to processes and activities and are used to assign costs to an activity cost pool by measuring the quantity of resources utilised by a process or activity. Activity drivers map activities to cost objects and are used to attribute activity cost pools to the ultimate cost objects.

In a financial institution, usually the same delivery channel or unit provides widely different financial products and services that typically consume very different types and amounts of resources. On the other hand, over time more and more of such businesses use shared services and systems. Therefore, it is a very complex and time-consuming task to analyse activities and cost drivers through a maze of mapping and attribution. In implementing ABC for the first time, it is helpful to create what is known as a *cost flow diagram*. The time-consuming part, of course comes after that in which cost analysts break out identifiable processes and interview the service providers as to how much of their weekly time and effort goes towards a unit of each activity. The unit cost of most resources requires less effort.

Kocakulah and Diekman (2001) provide a detailed example of implementation of ABC in a commercial lending set-up, in which the *cost drivers* for the commercial lending department are: (a) loan application, closing and setup; (b) ability to draw and advance funds (revolving capacity) on the loan; (c) method of payment; and (d) required account maintenance.

By focusing on processes, ABC forces a financial institution to dissect its activities in order to obtain efficiencies through process improvement and to consolidate tasks in providing services and conducting business. Process re-engineering and error reduction, either as a one-time or as a "continuous improvement" project (referred to as six-sigma, as popularised by Motorola and General Electric), has come to the forefront recently in financial institutions. ABC aligns financial accounting and strategic decision-making with those efforts.

As with any analytical methodology, ABC simply provides improved data to the decision makers in financial metric form. It is up to them as to how the information is used and for what purposes. Most financial institutions look at ABC as a tool for understanding and reducing costs and for process improvements. Such efficiency and cost reduction is only half the story, even with the much heralded concepts of six-sigma and continuous improvement. To derive full benefit, the tools of ABC must be used by financial institutions for more accurate expense allocations in performance measurement and pricing.

ACTIVITY-BASED COSTING AND SIMULATION

There are valid reasons why service industries in general and financial institutions in particular have been late adopters of ABC. Compared to traditional manufacturing processes, service processes are much more variable because people are so directly involved in the process flow. It is often difficult to obtain precise estimates of resource utilization and even activity flows. Managers and employees interviewed by accounting analysts are not in a position to state exact values when describing how much time or other effort is attached to particular process or activity. The precision is not as much one of measurement (whether mentally or by use of a stopwatch for example) as of the inherent randomness in the processes themselves in a service organisation with its significant human elements.

Randomness is talked of in the context of probability distribution of a variable being measured. Traditional accountants find it very difficult to deal with probability distributions. Instead, it is not uncommon to insist on a single "point estimate." Such estimates may be considered as expected or median values. ABC has the element of process redesign and improvement as its objective, in addition to better allocation of expenses. Understanding the consequences of process changes is very important. The cost flow diagram (referred to in the last section) is a first step in ABC since it provides understanding the overall nature of an existing business process or activity. Creating a cost flow diagram with point estimates is of limited use in understanding process changes and their impact on cost and performance.

Higher order statistics like range (maximum minus minimum), standard deviation or certain percentile values all together provide a much better understanding of a process or activity than does the expected value. One way of capturing such aspects of uncertainty is to use *simulation modelling tools*. Computer simulation enables building of scenarios consistent with the uncertainty in complicated business processes that are inherently imprecise. It is beyond the scope of this chapter to provide a detailed description of a simulation-based ABC. The reader is referred to Swane and Gladwin (1998) for details as well as an example of the benefits of simulation-based ABC in the case of a telephone support center at a mortgage bank.

Simulation provides capability of taking into account the dynamic nature of the processes as they get realised over time as well the random nature of the processes. The simulation process can also take into account well-specified behavioral elements (of both customers and employees) into the computation. Simulation softwares typically provide animation capability that allows us to see how people and information flow through the system. This animation is a great facilitator for the business manager to see whether the ABC set-up is an accurate representation of the business process and provide quite an accurate sanity check, without having to try to understand some of the statistical elements. Simulation-based ABC facilitates sensitivity analyses and "what-if" analyses of both costs and performances, preparing the way for much more well-informed decision making. Finally, it also provides a relatively inexpensive way of doing ABC analysis to compare future systems.

While ABC implementation is more complex than usual in a financial institution, by the time the technique came along in financial institutions, some parts of financial institutions, dealing with contingent valuations, had already been familiar with Monte Carlo simulation techniques and setting up of models that are essentially simulated by a computer software. Therefore, simulation-based ABC is not only more suitable for financial institutions but also starts with a minimum level of familiarity.

EXPENSE ALLOCATION TO EACH PRODUCT AND PRICING

Pricing of a product such that the institution is adequately compensated for the costs incurred and risks taken is a basic day-to-day function performed in a financial institution. All life-time positive and negative cash flows expected of the product and their timings need to be taken into account (ex-ante) as well as the attributed economic capital at different points of the product's life. For most products, the actual expenses in originating, maintaining, servicing and collections (if there is delinquency or default) are not uniform though the product's life-time. In fact they vary considerably across different points of the product's life. In a pricing model in large financial institutions, economic capital and cost of funds (FTP) are incorporated in rather sophisticated ways. Yet it is rare to have expenses incorporated in a way that varies from point-to-point of the product's lifetime.

There is a reason for lack of sophistication in capturing expenses in pricing models. Until recently, expenses or costs were tracked based on general ledger charts of account. In all the three allocation approaches mentioned in the previous section, the profit centre may be a general ledger hierarchy point or a business unit or a geographic branch location. Not very often is it a product or a portfolio of similar products. A profit centre or an organisation point in a general ledger hierarchy in a typical bank consists of several fundamentally different product types (the simplest example is loans and deposits) and widely different size of product within each product category. An expense allocation methodology based primarily on general ledger hierarchy provides an average picture completely inadequate for differentiated product pricing in a world of reducing margins in a competitive market.

Activity-based costing or ABC introduced in the last section focuses on processes. The way in which these processes are studied is not necessarily looking at processes that constitute the origination and maintenance of a product. ABC processes are in the

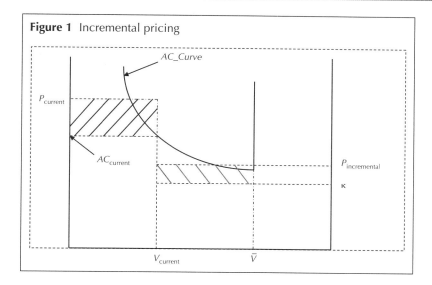

Figure 1 Incremental pricing

context of an activity and one activity in a financial institution often supports parts of the expenses on many products with different characteristics, including size.

FIXED VERSUS VARIABLE COSTS AND INCREMENTAL PRICING

The distinction between fixed and variable cost in economics is that fixed cost is the same irrespective of the number of units produced and variable cost is an increasing function of volume. Of course, fixed cost is fixed only for a certain range of volume till capacity utilisation reaches full-capacity and significant costs are incurred to produce beyond that volume level. Let F be the fixed cost and $G(v) = \kappa * v$ be the variable cost as a function of production volume v. F is fixed for the range $0 \leq v \leq \bar{V}$. Then total cost is $F + G(v)$ and the unit or average cost $AC(v)$ is $\kappa + (F/v)$ in the range $0 \leq v \leq \bar{V}$. Figure 1 depicts unit cost as a function of v:

The current profit is $(P_{current} - AC_{current}) * v_{current}$ depicted by the rectangle shaded by black lines. The current price covers all fixed and variable costs and leaves a profit. Increase in volume does not increase fixed cost (up to $\bar{V}$) but only affects variable cost. Thus new production can be priced at some level lower than $P_{current}$ and as long as it is higher than the variable cost (κ = variable cost per unit), the bank makes a profit. Setting such a price for new production is called *incremental pricing*. The bank can continue to set incremental prices *temporarily* until the volume hits $\bar{V}$ after which the fixed cost is no longer F but much higher as significant investment is needed to produce any further beyond the full-capacity volume. The additional profit is depicted by the lower shaded rectangle.

Incremental pricing is *temporary* in another sense. The price level depicted by $P_{current}$ which fully covers the fixed cost is applicable as long as the current product is on the books of the bank. Most bank products amortise and the "current" volume is replaced by "new production" in a continuous state of flux. Over the years, the weighted average life of a typical bank product has only come down. If incremental pricing concept is applied to all new production for a prolonged period, soon there will be no volume that will cover fixed costs. Clearly this is not tenable. Incremental pricing can be used over a *short period* in which strategically the bank wants to gain market share, perhaps to cross-sell other products and services to the newly acquired customers.

In general, the tendency to resort to some form of incremental pricing stems from taking a *marginal* perspective whether it is related to economic capital, funds transfer pricing or expense allocation. Sometimes it is the prevalent expense allocation methodology that provides incentives for pricing behaviour by the business units.

FULL-ABSORPTION COSTING VERSUS CAPACITY-BASED COSTING

In traditional costing (even activity based costing) the total cost of a shared system is looked upon with no reference to capacity utilisation. This can be described as *full-absorption costing*. The underlying concept of full-absorption costing is that, at the present moment, the unused capacity is an actual cost incurred irrespective of whether it is utilised or not. As utilisation increases or decreases, it will be reflected in the next period's expense allocation.

Full-absorption costing essentially divides expense pools by a volume statistic to arrive at a unit cost. It does not have a time dimension. In contrast, *capacity-based costing* introduces capacity measurement, capacity utilisation and available unused capacity into the cost allocation methodology. The calculation incorporates these in the form of a *time dimension*. Capacity-based costing and

ABC are not two mutually exclusive methodologies. Estimating the time required to perform a transactional activity and using it as an integral part of the activity analysis was introduced as a modification of ABC by Kaplan and Cooper (1998). Also see Kaplan and Anderson (2004) for more recent development of time-driven ABC and a very lucid numerical example.

In the context of product pricing (and pricing of potential acquisition of an institution or a portfolio), the dichotomy between full-absorption costing and capacity-based costing has an interesting aspect. Inclusion of unused capacity will always overstate unit cost. This translates to a higher pricing and (in a competitive market) a lower volume. Incorporating unused capacity in the costing calculation enables somewhat lower pricing and consequently a higher volume, which in turn, increases capacity utilisation and reduces true cost. A dramatic increase in capacity utilisation and decrease in true cost can happen when a complete portfolio is added through acquisition. Full-absorption costing prevents the institution from aggressive bidding by taking into account potential increase in capacity utilisation and reduction in true unit cost if the portfolio is acquired. In case of decisions on sale of portfolios, potential decrease in capacity utilisation and consequent increase in unit cost, if the sale goes through, may not be taken into account in the price negotiations.

When it comes to pricing products on a day-to-day basis, the result is not so clear cut. The current lack of capacity utilisation is an actual cost that the institution has to bear. Each product does *not* have a significant impact on the level of utilisation, at the margin. A simpler full-absorption costing with regular revision as capacity utilisation (or any other aspect for that matter) goes up or down, gives a good enough picture. Capacity-based costing may be viewed as an enhancement of full-absorption costing rather than a competing methodology. It may be beneficial to take both a full-absorption costing and a capacity-based costing perspective in expense allocation in a financial institution. Of course, the downside is the need for more accountants and analysts. Capacity-based costing works best and pays the most dividends in areas which have a high volume of transaction processing.

Both full-absorption costing and capacity-based costing have their pros and cons. See Spaller and McDonald (2003) for a full enumeration of the pros and cons and explanations. Clearly, full-absorption costing is easier and less staff-intensive to implement and maintain. Capacity-based costing requires more detailed analysis of the resources used in the so-called "production" sites (although in a financial institution, the resources in the "production" sites are actually providing service rather than producing). Capacity-based costing facilitates active communication between service providers and service users and supports resource management throughout the organisation. Following the widespread introduction of technology and automated processes in the last 15 years, financial institutions have started focusing on "continuous improvement" – a concept introduced by Edward Deming in the Japanese manufacturing industry. Such process improvements have immediate impact on performance measures and pricing in a capacity-based costing paradigm.

ARM'S-LENGTH TRANSFER PRICING OF EXPENSES

A relatively new concept of expense allocation is to utilise the *arm's length principle*: that is, the expense computation is based on the price that would have occurred in a transaction had it occurred between independent parties. Such a price is referred to as *transfer price*. Clearly, no price is observed in connection with an internal company transaction for example a service provided by one centre A to another centre B in the same financial institution. However, if centre B were to acquire the same service in an arms length transaction with a third party, a transfer price would have been observed.

Since funds transfer pricing (based on observed "opportunity cost" or "price" of funds) has long been prevalent in financial institutions, it is natural for banks to embrace transfer pricing of expenses. In order to improve efficiency in their internal service providers, some companies have even allowed business units to exercise the alternative of getting the service from an outside provider, if that happens to be cheaper. But this is easier said than done. Without actually finalising the procurement of a service by going through the request-for-proposal and negotiation processes, the observed price in the market is rarely for the "same" service as provided by the internal support centre.

Arm's-length transfer pricing is not inconsistent with costing approaches introduced in earlier sections. It can be considered a variant of ABC. Many of the more well-defined activities in ABC can have readily observable market price. Costing for those activities or sub-activities can rely on transfer pricing while those for other activities can follow usual ABC techniques. Arm's-length transfer pricing of expenses, where dependable, brings considerable objectivity to the expense allocation process.

CONCLUSION

Expense allocation is one of the three legs of modern performance measurement in a financial institution. The other two are funds transfer pricing and economic capital. The methodologies of expense allocation are less analytical than the methodologies of funds transfer pricing and economic capital. But it is the most labour-intensive. Costing as a sub-discipline in financial accounting has been in existence for decades. Dissatisfaction with traditional costing in the 1980s has led to new ways of costing and expense allocation. One of the major developments is activity-based costing or ABC, which is progressively being adopted by all companies for better control of costs and better resource management.

More than companies in other industries, financial institutions have diverse financial products delivered from a single hierarchical unit and different units dependent on shared services and systems. Therefore, an accurate expense allocation methodology is necessarily elaborate and complex in a financial institution. Since financial institutions have very high expense ratios, the very magnitude of expense items in any performance measure elevates the importance of expense allocation in a financial institution.

Economic capital and funds transfer pricing are concepts and methodologies that have been developed specifically for financial institutions. They are rarely discussed outside the context of financial institutions. Established expense allocation methodologies, on the other hand, are not specific to financial institutions. This chapter provides brief introductions to ABC and capacity-based costing, which are only now gaining ground in financial institutions. These are topics in themselves applicable to financial accounting in all companies and the reader needs to study the references for detailed expositions and numerical examples. The chapter briefly discusses direct allocation, sequential allocation and simultaneous allocation as the three broad approaches of expense allocation which are also common to financial accounting of all companies.

Most of the contents of the chapter have focused on specific issues of performance measurement and pricing in the context of a financial institution. Expense allocation may be important for purposes of minimising costs and managing resources. But it is equally important for purposes of performance measurement, customer profitability and pricing.

1   A contribution margin of US$2,300 and a net income of US$780 in a year for a SME loan of size US$100,000 is not at all uncommon in a competitive market. It will certainly not be considered a marginal transaction.

REFERENCES

Kaplan, R. S. and S. R. Anderson, 2004, "Time-Driven Activity-based Costing," *Harvard Business Review*, **82(11)**, pp 131–8.

Kaplan, R. S. and R. Cooper, 1998, *Cost & Effect: Using Integrated Cost Systems to Drive Profitability and Performance*, Boston, MA: Harvard Business School Press, pp 296–9.

Kocakulah, M. C. and D. Diekman, 2001, "Implementing activity-based costing (ABC) to measure commercial loan profitability," *The Journal of Bank Cost & Management Accounting*.

Smith, J. T. and C. Harper, 2001, "Bank Cost Analysis Model (BCAM): implementing activity-based cost management in a financial institution," *The Journal of Bank Cost & Management Accounting*.

Spaller, R. and R. McDonald, 2003, "Capacity-based costing in banking," *The Journal of Bank Cost & Management Accounting*.

5

From Traditional to Risk-Adjusted Measures of Internal Business Unit Performance

INTRODUCTION

Chapter 1 enumerated traditional and risk-adjusted performance measures at the *corporate* level reported by financial institutions in their annual reports as part of their balance sheet, income statement or off-balance sheet. Most finance professionals in a financial institution, however, occupy their time with *internal* business unit (or even product level) performance measures. Contrasted with corporate measures, which are predicated by GAAP, internal business unit performance measures also depend, often critically, on one or more internal methodology. This fact adds a whole new complexity not encountered while dealing with corporate performance measures. As in Chapter 1, the purpose is to define precisely the more important financial performance measures used for internal performance measurement, monitoring and review.

The three broad categories of internal methodologies that are critical to business unit performance measures are: funds transfer pricing, economic capital allocation and expense allocation. First, internal methodologies, by definition, are not mandated by any formal standards or legal requirements. Second, the results of internal methodologies are not observed in the market although they may use some market observed variables to calibrate. The fundamentals of funds transfer pricing, economic capital allocation and expense allocation have been introduced and discussed in Chapters 2, 3 and 4 respectively. Although the concepts and basic methodologies presented in those chapters are now fairly standardised across the financial institutions, in terms of details each institution can choose from among several possibilities, which will give somewhat different results.

Segment (public) reporting is a relatively new development in the financial industry. In the second part of the chapter we critically examine issues in segment reporting and the pros and cons of comparing internal performance measures across business units and across institutions.

TRADITIONAL BUSINESS UNIT PERFORMANCE MEASURES

The primary function of a financial institution is financial intermediation. Financial intermediation, in its basic form, refers to borrowing funds from one group (of individuals typically) at one rate and lending funds to another group (of businesses typically) at a different rate. The financial intermediary makes money by creating a "spread gap" between the borrowing and lending rates. It is no surprise, therefore, that two of the oldest performance measures for a financial institution are *net interest income* and *net interest margin*. FTP has already been introduced in Chapter 2 in some detail. It is necessary to first arrive at the FTP rate for an asset or a liability in order to compute net interest margin and net interest income. The FTP rate depends on the vintage, that is the time at which the asset or the liability was originated (more particularly, the interest rate yield curve at the time of origination), the amortisation of the principal of the asset or liability and any optionality, like prepayment.

Net interest margin and net interest income

$$NIM_{asset} = Coupon - FTP\_rate$$

$$NIM_{liability} = FTP\_rate - Rate\_paid$$

$$NII_{BU} = \sum_{assets}^{all} [Coupon_i - FTP\_rate_i] * A_i$$
$$+ \sum_{liabilities}^{all} [FTP\_rate_j - Rate\_paid_j] * L_j$$

where FTP_rate_i is the funds transfer pricing rate (not dollar amount) charged for a financial (earning) asset with balance A_i and is the funds transfer pricing rate credited for a financial liability with balance L_j.

$$NIM_{BU} = \frac{NII_{BU}}{\sum\limits_{assets}^{all} A_i}$$

Business unit revenue

$$Revenue_{BU} = NI_{BU} + Fee_{BU}$$

Business unit contribution margin

The most common traditional performance measure for a business unit in a commercial or retail bank is contribution margin (CM). The business unit has assets with balance A_i, $i = 1$ to I and liabilities with balance L_j, $j = 1$ to J. It is important to keep in mind that, unlike at the corporate level, the balance sheet of a business unit *need not balance*. Therefore, one cannot say that: assets = liabilities + owners' equity for a business unit. There is nothing wrong with that since we are only concerned with *internal* performance measurements in this chapter. But it is important to realise, at this stage, that one cannot expect some of the internal performance ratios to behave the same way or even be of similar magnitude as corporate level performance ratios.

Let EC_i be the economic capital (equity portion) associated with the asset with balance A_i. Then the debt portion is $D_i = A_i - EC_i$, which can be expressed as $D_i = (1 - \lambda_i) * A_i$ where $\lambda_i = EC_i/A_i$. Then contribution margin of the assets in the business unit can be defined as

$$CM_{Assets} = \sum\limits_{assets}^{all} [Coupon_j - FTP\_rate_i * (1 - \lambda_i)] * A_i$$
$$+ Fee_{Assets} - Dir\_Exp_{Assets} - EL_{Assets}$$

Contribution margin of the liabilities in the business unit (there is no "debt portion" for a liability) can be defined as:

$$CM_{Liabilities} = \sum_{liabilities}^{all} [FTP\_rate_j - Rate\_paid_j] * L_j$$
$$+ Fee_{Liabilities} - Dir\_Exp_{Liabilities} - EL_{Liabilities}$$

$$CM_{BU} = CM_{Assets} + CM_{Liabilities}$$

Ex-post, we can replace EL by actual $Loss$ in the period.

A much less prevalent business unit performance measure is business unit Net Income:

$$NI_{BU} = (1 - tax\_rate) * [CM_{BU} - Overhead\_Exp_{BU}]$$

Expense ratio

$$Expense\_Ratio_{BU} = \frac{Dir\_Exp_{BU} + Overhead\_Exp_{BU}}{Revenue_{BU}}$$

Non-performing loans ratio

$$NPL\_Ratio_{BU} = \frac{Balance\_of\_Non\_performing\_Loans_{BU}}{Balance\_of\_All\_Loans_{BU}}$$

Net charge-off

$$NCO_{BU} = \frac{Balance\_of\_Loans\_charged\_off_{BU}}{Balance\_of\_All\_Loans_{BU}}$$

RISK-ADJUSTED BUSINESS UNIT PERFORMANCE MEASURES

Of the three legs of performance measurement in a financial institution, EC is the most analytical and came into existence most recently. Chapter 3 provides the fundamentals of economic capital. In industry parlance, risk-adjusted performance measure has become synonymous with performance measure that takes EC into account.

$$EC_{BU} = EC_{BU}(credit) + EC_{BU}(market)$$
$$+ EC_{BU}(operational) + EC_{BU}(strategic)$$

$$EC_{BU} = \sum_{assets}^{all} EC_i * A_i + \sum_{liabilities}^{all} EC_j * L_j$$

Return on risk-adjusted capital (RORAC)

Since economic capital is a measure of risk, it is already risk-adjusted. The ratio of net income to economic capital is essentially RORAC:

$$RORAC_{BU} = \frac{NI_{BU}}{EC_{BU}}$$

RORAC and RAROC are often used interchangeably. However, this chapter makes a purposeful distinction by defining RAROC as follows.

Risk-adjusted return on capital (RAROC)

$$RAROC_{BU} = \frac{NI_{BU} - k * EC_{BU}}{EC_{BU}}$$

where k is the institution's cost of equity or required return on equity (see Chapter 3 on Economic Capital Fundamentals as to how k is determined).

Economic profit (EP)

As mentioned in Chapters 1 and 3, the most common risk-adjusted performance measure is EP or EVA or SVA as it is variously known.

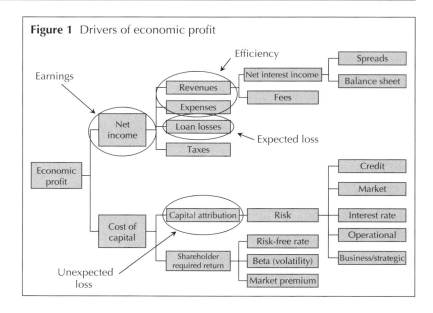

Figure 1 Drivers of economic profit

The concept was originally introduced by the economist Alfred Marshall in the 1890s, applied in General Motors in the 1920s and later popularised by Stern-Stewart in the 1980s. It gained acceptance in the financial industry in the 1990s.

$$EP_{BU} = NI_{BU} - k * EC_{BU}$$

The following figure depicts the drivers of economic profit. Many of the drivers are traditional measures well-known to finance professionals in a financial institution. Economic capital is still a fairly new concept and introduces most of the complexity in the measurement of EP.

PERIOD PERFORMANCE VERSUS VINTAGE PERFORMANCE

Readers may realise that all the performance measures reported in Chapter 1 and in this chapter so far are performance over a period of one month, one quarter or one year and in some cases the value at the end of the period. This can generally be called "period performance" in contrast to "vintage performance". Vintage refers to the time at which an asset or a liability or an off-balance sheet item was originated. Vintage performance is the performance of all transactions originated at a particular vintage.

It is important to understand the implications of the distinction between: (a) period performance, ie performance measures over a short period $\tau + t$ to $\tau + t + 1$ across all vintages τ; and (b) performance measures for a particular vintage τ. First of all, in any period, they are not likely to be similar, let alone the same. Yet such divergence causes considerable misgivings for those used to traditional financial accounting.

It is not uncommon for banks to tighten credit underwriting at the beginning and through a recession. It is also associated with charging higher price for credit even though demand may be soft. This results in low origination or new production but at a better risk-adjusted return. At the same time, the existing portfolio is deteriorating leading to higher economic capital, higher *NPL* and *NCO*. The life-time risk-adjusted performance measures for new production are higher than or near normal while the single-period risk-adjusted performance measures for the portfolio are (much) lower than normal. This, usually baffling, divergence of the two types of performance measures at times of credit cycle downturn is at the root of many a misunderstanding when non-traditional performance measures are introduced for the first time at such a downturn.

Another source of much confusion among finance professionals is also related to the credit cycle. At the downturn, the credit deterioration of the portfolio increases the economic capital. No doubt the defaulted loans consume a lot of economic capital. But the loans which have deteriorated but not defaulted (in regulatory terminology, criticised and classified loans) are much larger in number and overall consume more economic capital in dollar terms. Most of these loans recover as the credit cycle improves and the economic capital drops several times. During this credit cycle, these loans are still in accrual status and do not impact traditional business unit performance measures like contribution margin significantly. However, the performance measures like business unit economic profit or return on risk-adjusted capital go through huge fluctuations as the credit cycle first deteriorates and then improves again. In percentage terms, such fluctuations can be just as much as fluctuations in *NPL* or *NCO* as the credit cycle moves through the trough. The latter is not surprising, nor should the former.

PEER GROUP COMPARISON

Financial institutions seem to have an obsession with comparing their performance with a number of other institutions, the so-called "peer group". This makes common sense as long as, conceptually, the performance measures are comparable across institutions. Most corporate level traditional performance measures (discussed in Chapter 1) are generally comparable across institutions. Accountants and analysts, used to traditional corporate performance measures, therefore, find it valuable to do peer group comparison. But what happens when, conceptually, the performance measures are not comparable across institutions?

Corporate level non-traditional performance measures are also generally comparable across institutions if some care is taken to look for possible sources of inconsistency. That is why issues of peer group comparison were not discussed in Chapter 1. The problem arises when one compares internal business unit performance measures across different financial institutions. This is true of both traditional and risk-adjusted business unit performance measures.

It is evident from the definitions of business unit performance measures that they are critically dependent on variables like FTP_rate_i, EC_i, λ_i and *Overhead_Exp* etc, all of which are derived as a result of internal methodologies. The calculated values of internal business unit performance measures, whether traditional or risk-adjusted, can change significantly as any of these variables change. By definition, the values of internal variables like funds transfer pricing rate for a product or economic capital attributed to a transaction or expense allocated to a product are not observable. It must also be evident to the readers of Chapters 2, 3 and 4 that internal methodologies across financial institutions, though conceptually similar, may vary considerably in details. As a result, values of business unit performance measures can be quite different across financial institutions.

In recent years some financial institutions have started providing performance of business units or segments in their annual reports. Segment reporting is becoming more and more common among publicly traded financial institutions. Unlike corporate level performance measures, those of the segments are subject to internal methodologies for funds transfer pricing, economic capital allocation and expense allocation. As stated above, the details of these internal methodologies may vary considerably across financial institutions. Such differences are not necessarily those of true performance but arise from different (internal) ways of arriving at the same business unit performance measure.

There is another reason, sometimes an even more serious one, why segment reports are not necessarily comparable across financial institutions. How internal business units (with similar nomenclature) are organised may vary considerably from institution to institution. Often the hierarchy is determined by historical happenstance or the preferences of certain individuals. It is not uncommon for some businesses or products being moved from one segment to another once every few years – this is done for other considerations with no attention paid to the effects on business unit performance reporting. This effect usually does not cause problems with comparing traditional business unit performance measures across institutions. But comparing risk-adjusted business unit performance measures across institutions is another matter altogether.

We will provide one simple instance of how a business unit performance can be widely different across different financial institutions depending on how the business unit is organised. In this simple instance, the only difference is core deposits relative to assets. Consider a "corporate and investment banking" segment, which most financial institutions report as a segment. The "corporate and investment banking" segment typically will have core deposits in the form of demand deposits. Some banks may include middle-market lending as part of the segment and others may not. As a result the relative size of core deposits to assets can vary from as low as 10% to as high as 50%. Unlike a corporation, a business unit does not have a balanced (ie, assets = liabilities + owners equity) balance sheet.

Assets (money lent or promised to others by the financial institution) have significant credit risk while liabilities (money received by the financial institution from others) have none. Liabilities as well as assets have operational risk. Credit risk economic capital is typically much higher than operational risk economic capital. As a result assets typically attract much more economic capital per dollar than do liabilities, sometimes as much as five times. Core deposits, however, generate margins which are similar to margins of the assets. Therefore, if a "corporate and investment banking" unit of a bank has very low core deposits to assets ratio. Similarly, the "retail" business unit may have very different proportion of core deposits to consumer assets. A bank with a "retail" business where core deposits to consumer assets is very high will report a much higher segment RORAC than a bank with core deposits relatively small in comparison with consumer assets accounted for in the "retail" business unit. The appendix provides a table illustrating this point with representative numbers.

Bank analysts and most finance personnel of financial institutions commonly do peer group comparison from various angles. This is perfectly legitimate when they are comparing the corporate level performance of financial institutions in the peer group, at least most cases. Extrapolating the practice to peer group comparison in terms of segment or business unit performance is routinely fraught with danger.

CONCLUSION

Internal business unit performance measures in a financial institution are vital to monitoring performance and review. These measures are dependent on internal methodologies. The three legs of internal performance measures are funds transfer pricing, economic capital allocation and expense allocation. The internal methodologies need to be economically fair and generally transparent so that the business units, whose performances are being measured, view them as fair and objective.

The risk-adjusted performance measures at the business unit level tend to align business unit managers' objectives with a shareholder value creation paradigm. There is only one share price for the corporation as a whole; there is no share price observed for each business unit. To ensure that the actions of the business units add shareholder value increase share price for the corporation, the business unit performance measure must be (a) rolled up from business units to the corporate level relatively easily; and (b) closely aligned to share price. Economic profit is one such performance measure.

By definition, the values of internal variables like funds transfer pricing rate for a product or economic capital attributed to a transaction or expense allocated to a product are not observable. Internal methodologies across financial institutions, though conceptually similar, may vary considerably in details. This is one reason why internal business unit performances across financial institutions may not be comparable. The other reason, an even more serious one, is that the way in which internal business units (with similar nomenclature) are organised may vary considerably from institution to institution. As a result it is dangerous to compare business unit performance across different financial institutions.

Peer group comparison of performance is almost an obsession in the financial industry. Finance professionals, including CFOs, of financial institutions need to be careful and understand the pitfalls before embarking on a peer group comparison of business unit performance measures, particularly the non-traditional ones. More and more financial institutions are publicly reporting business unit performance in recent years. Bank analysts, used to peer group comparison of corporate level performance, also need to exercise the same caution before making comparisons routinely from such segment reporting of different financial institutions.

APPENDIX

In the following table we consider "retail" business units of four hypothetical banks. For simplicity we have only considered loans and deposits and only interest income

	Size (US$ mm)	NIM (bps)	NII (US$ mm)	Expenses (US$ mm)	Provisions (US$ mm)	EBT (US$ mm)	EC (US$ mm)	RORAC (%)
Retail BU of Bank 1								
Loans	5,000	420	210	90	60	60	300	13.00
Deposits	50,000	320	1,600	1,250	0	350	500	45.50
			1,810	1,340	60	410	800	**33.31**
Retail BU of Bank 2								
Loans	10,000	420	420	180	120	120	600	13.00
Deposits	50,000	320	1,600	1,250	0	350	500	45.50
			2,020	1,430	120	470	1,100	**27.77**
Retail BU of Bank 3								
Loans	40,000	420	1,680	720	480	480	2,400	13.00
Deposits	50,000	320	1,600	1,250	0	350	500	45.50
			3,280	1,970	480	830	2,900	**18.60**
Retail BU of Bank 4								
Loans	40,000	420	2,520	1,080	720	720	3,600	13.00
Deposits	50,000	320	1,600	1,250	0	350	500	45.50
			4,120	2,330	720	1,070	4,100	**16.96**

NIM = Net interest margin; NII = Net interest income; EBT = Earnings before tax; Provisions = Loan loss provision; EC = Economic capital; RORAC = Return on risk-adjusted capital

6

Risk-Adjusted Performance of Credit Products and Credit-Based Relationships

INTRODUCTION

One of the most common traditional functions of a financial institution has been the business of taking credit risk. Credit products have, over time, become more and more complex well beyond the simple traditional senior secured or unsecured loans. Credit underwriters have always taken the default risk of an individual loan by analysing the financial strength of the borrower (company or consumer). Accounting in financial institutions has long required provision for loan loss by creating a reserve account. Treasury functions of most banks have, for many years, a funds transfer pricing mechanism, which charges a cost of (borrowed) funds, taking into account the interest rate risk in the loan. Thus traditional pricing and performance measurement of the most common credit products have not been altogether devoid of risk perspectives. What has been lacking is a portfolio credit risk perspective, which affects unexpected losses that cannot be covered by reserves or from income. This is particularly important for wholesale lending since business cycles have long periodicity; large unexpected losses occur once in many years but such unexpected losses are many times higher in magnitude than losses in normal years. In the banking industry, the methodology to capture such unexpected losses that has come to be best practice is the concept of economic capital. Chapter 3 introduced the basic concepts of economic capital. This chapter will be restricted to credit risk economic capital only.

Pricing and performance measurement of a credit product involves much more than computing credit risk economic capital. Obviously, it has to take into account variable and fixed (overhead) expenses associated with underwriting, monitoring, collections, systems costs, maintenance of building and shared services. Since banks fund most of their assets with borrowed money, an elaborate funds transfer pricing mechanism is required to compute cost of funds that get incorporated in pricing and performance measurement. Chapter 2 introduced the basic concepts of funds transfer pricing.

A less obvious reason is that most banks often view a commercial credit product as part of a relationship with other (existing or potential) credit and non-credit products while taking pricing decisions. Therefore, performance in general has to be looked upon from the perspective of single credit product as well as the perspective of a relationship. In recent years, retail loans in traditional banks (less so in mono-line financial institutions) are progressively being viewed as part of an overall customer relationship.

The relationship typically includes off balance sheet products, most common of which are lines of credit (commercial drawal facilities, home equity lines of credit, etc). Funds transfer pricing charge does not apply to off balance sheet items and only takes effect when part or whole of the line is drawn. On the other hand, economic capital applies to off balance sheet items and is driven primarily by how much of the line is expected to be drawn when the borrower is going towards default.

BROAD TYPES OF ECONOMIC CAPITAL MODELS FOR CREDIT RISK

There are three fundamental approaches to modelling economic capital for credit risk: *intensity-based models*, *structural models* and *empirical models*. Intensity-based models describe default as an unpredictable event and do not assume any economic reason for default. They are based on a stochastic process called *intensity of default*, which describes the instantaneous probability of default. Correlation between default events is described by the correlation between intensity processes. Empirical models are based on econometric estimation from historical data. Structural models, on the other hand, describe default as an event that arises from the financial situation of the borrower. The first useful structural model of default is described in the seminal work of Robert Merton (1974). Merton assumes that a firm has a stock and a single non-amortising debt obligation. The firm's asset value is described by a geometric Brownian motion. The firm defaults if, at maturity of the debt, the value of the firm's assets falls below the face value of the debt. Stock price in the Merton model is a call option on the firm's assets with the debt face value being the option strike price. Many refinements and extensions of the Merton model have subsequently appeared both from academic and practitioners" perspectives. All of these structural models are based on Merton's framework and are often called Merton-type models.

From the economic capital perspective, the most valuable adaptation of Merton's model has been offered by Oldrich Vasicek (1987, 1991). Vasicek applied Merton's model to a portfolio of borrowers. As in Merton's model, each borrower is characterised by a lognormal asset-value process. A borrower defaults when the individual or organisation's asset value falls below a threshold defined by its liabilities. Correlations between borrowers" defaults arise from correlation between their asset values. Correlations between asset values, in turn, are described by a common dependence of asset returns on a single systematic factor, representing the state of the economy. Thus the asset return for each borrower has a systematic component, reflecting the effect of the economy on the borrower, and an idiosyncratic component, describing fortunes and misfortunes unique for the borrower. Assuming homogeneous portfolio of loans with zero recoveries, Vasicek derived the distribution function for the portfolio loss. The Vasicek model has also been refined and extended to include non-homogeneous portfolios and non-zero stochastic recoveries. The term "Vasicek model" is often used to include these extensions of the original Vasicek model.

To describe different systematic effects for firms belonging to different industries and/or different geographical regions, the single systematic factor in the Vasicek model is replaced by a set of correlated systematic factors. This multi-factor extension of the Vasicek model lies in the foundation of such industry models as KMV's PortfolioManager and RiskMetrics CreditMetrics. However, CSFB's Credit Risk Plus, is not a Merton-type model.

The international Basel II capital adequacy rules for financial institutions were finalised in April 2003 by the Basel Committee for Banking Supervision (Basel 2001, 2003). At the core of the Basel II capital formulae is what has come to be known as the asymptotic single-risk factor framework (ASRF) model. Generally, while the expected loss from an asset depends only on the characteristics of the asset itself, its contributory economic capital additionally depends on properties of the portfolio where the asset is held. Michael Gordy (2003) has shown that the only case when the asset economic capital is independent of the portfolio composition is when: (a) the portfolio is infinitely fine-grained (ie, its largest exposure represents a negligible fraction of its total exposure); and (b) the portfolio losses are driven by a single systematic risk factor. These two conditions constitute the ASRF framework. Under the first condition, all the idiosyncratic risk in the portfolio is diversified away and the asymptotic portfolio loss equals the expected loss conditional on the systematic risk factors. The second condition causes the portfolio loss to be a deterministic monotonic function of the single systematic factor. Therefore, the portfolio economic capital equals its expected loss conditional on the systematic risk factor being equal to the percentile corresponding to the level of confidence. Due to the linearity of the expectation operator, contributory economic capital of an asset is nothing but the expected loss on this asset conditional on the appropriate value of the systematic risk factor.

TYPES OF CREDIT RISK IN A FINANCIAL INSTITUTION

Over the last 20 years, credit risk models that have been developed primarily focused on corporate bonds and portfolio of senior loans, for which adequate default data are available. Financial institutions, however, have progressively created assets that are significantly different in credit characteristics (including structure, seniority) from senior loans but at the same time have considerable credit risk. The following paragraphs will briefly enumerate the different types of credit risks in a financial institution. A portfolio view will be taken rather than a transaction view.

Credit risk in senior lending

The risk of loss of principal due to default of a borrower of senior loans made by the financial institution or change in value of the loan due to migration in credit quality of the borrower. The economic capital for the former is referred to as default-mode capital, while the economic capital for the latter (or sometimes both together) is referred to as marked-to-market-mode capital. Credit risk also includes similar risk in lines of credit and letters of credit issued to potential borrowers. The main drivers of default-mode credit risk economic capital are the exposure at default, the borrower's probability of default, the loss given default (ie, severity of loss if default happens), the correlation of the exposure to other exposures in the portfolio, correlation between the default event and loss given default (since in an economic downturn asset values are typically depressed, reducing recovery). To calculate marked-to-market mode economic capital, the remaining maturity of the loan and transition probabilities as well as market credit spreads are the main drivers. The concept of economic capital was first applied to credit risk in corporate and retail portfolios. There are numerous models and analysis for economic capital for credit risk, some of which are mentioned in the next section of this chapter.

Counterparty credit risk

Counterparty credit risk is the risk that a counterparty to a derivative trade may default before the final settlement of the derivative contract's cash flows. A loss occurs if the counterparty defaults while the derivative has a positive market value to the other party. Modelling of counterparty credit risk is more complex than modelling of credit risk first because of the bilateral nature of counterparty exposures and second, because the uncertainty comes from both the credit default event of the counterparty and the market value of the derivative contract. A recent model developed by Ernst Canabarro, Evan Picoult and Tom Wilde (2003) captures the complexity of modelling counterparty credit risk.

Credit risk in securitisation

Securitisation consists of the transfer of a pool of loans to a special purpose vehicle and then selling the receivables to investors with specified priorities. Securitisations are generally classified as mortgage backed securities (MBS), asset-backed securities (ABS) or *collateralised* debt obligations (CDO). This prioritisation of payment makes the nature of credit risk different from that of loans or bonds. Ratings alone are not enough to determine the economic capital for credit risk in a securitisation tranche. Only recently have models for credit risk in securitisations developed by Michael Pykhtin and Ashish Dev (2002, 2003a) and Michael Gordy and David Jones (2003). These models show that the main drivers of economic capital for a securitisation tranche are its rating, the granularity of the underlying pool of loans, and the thickness of the tranche.

Credit risk in merchant banking

Merchant banking activities have distinct credit risk from that of senior lending. Typically they consist of mezzanine and equity participations with often availability of upside through warrants and more control over management of the borrower company. While it is recognised that economic capital requirements for merchant banking are many times higher than typical senior lending, there is no well-established model for economic capital for merchant banking.

Country risk in international banking

Loans to borrowers in a foreign country have risks due to actions by the foreign government, quite independent of the borrower's financial condition. It is generally possible to extend credit risk models to economic capital for country risk by incorporating sovereign default probability into the calculation. The modelling is essentially similar to credit risk economic capital models.

Residual value risk in leases

Leasing has progressively become a large business for many commercial banks and automobile "captive" financing companies. In addition to credit risk of default of the lessee, there is considerable risk in the residual value of the asset being less than the stated value as well as the uncertainty of whether or not the lessee decides to buy the asset at the stated residual value. A model developed by Michael Pykhtin and Ashish Dev (2003b) addresses the risks in auto lease residuals and the economic capital associated with such risk. Many of the characteristics of the model can be applied to residual risk in other kinds of leases.

PERFORMANCE MEASUREMENT OF A SINGLE CREDIT PRODUCT

Let us consider a senior loan with maturity T and initial balance of $B(0)$ and an amortising[1] balance of $B(t)$ at time t for $t = 1$ to T. In the special case of a pure bullet loan, $B(t) = B(0)$ for all t. The loan has a monthly coupon payment. The coupon may be fixed or floating and can be represented generally as $r_c(t)$ – same for all t if it is a fixed rate loan. In addition the loan may derive fee income at some point (typically in the beginning). Let $fee(t)$ be the fee at time t. For most t's $fee(t) = 0$.

The credit risk of a loan comes from its propensity to default resulting in the bank not being able to get the whole principal back. The exposure at default, EAD, is the maximum amount due to the bank when the loan defaults. For a loan EAD = Balance outstanding at default.

The probability of default or PD of the loan depends primarily on the ability to repay, in other words, on the financial strength of the underlying company or consumer. In addition to purely financial or economic variables, other non-economic factors also have a bearing on probability of default – for example, strength of management of a company or demographic characteristics of a customer. The relationship between PD and its drivers is usually determined by econometric estimation of a limited dependent variable. Examples of this methodology are Fair-Issac's consumer scores and Moody's RiskCalc. In case of companies with publicly available information, stock price and stock options, an estimated default frequency, EDF can be derived using an extension of the Merton framework that has been popularised by Moody's KMV. For the purposes of this chapter, we will treat EDF and PD as equivalent.

The loan may be secured by one or more assets or it may be unsecured. Also, there may be a guarantor who guarantees its repayment. These and other factors determine how much of the exposure (ie, outstanding balance) will be recovered if the obligor goes into default. This is usually captured by the variable LGD. Recoveries made at different points in time are usually present valued at an appropriate discount rate in estimating LGD. LGD is most commonly expressed as a percentage.

The expected loss for the loan is given by

$$EL(t) = EAD(t) * PD * LGD$$

The loan is considered as part of a portfolio of other senior loans. The economic capital attributable to the credit risk in the loan as part of a portfolio of loans is dependent on the correlation of default amongst the loans in the portfolio as well as on the probability of default and loss given default. The function $G[\ldots]$ is non-linear in general:

$$EC_{credit}(t) = EAD(t) * G[PD, LGD, Correlation]$$

A loan typically would have operational risk[2] which can be also measured in the same "currency" namely economic capital. This chapter will not go into the details of computing operational risk economic capital, $EC_{operational}$.

$$EC(t) = EC_{credit}(t) + EC_{operational}$$

The loan is funded partly by debt and partly by equity. The appropriate equity required to support the loan at origination is $EC(0)$. Let $D(0) = B(0) - EC(0)$ be the debt portion of the funding of the loan at origination. We can represent $D(0) = (1-\lambda) \times B(0)$ where $\lambda = EC(0)/B(0)$. Let τ represent the (calendar) vintage of the loan. It represents the market environment prevailing at the time the loan was originated. FTP is charged by the Treasury for each loan or asset based on the cost of funding the debt portion, which accounts for the interest rate risk in the loan. The cost of funds depends on the vintage of the loan. The dollar FTP charge at time t is the product of the FTP rate F_τ determined at inception and the current balance:

$$FTP(t) = F_\tau * (1-\lambda) * B(t)$$

F_τ depends on the prevailing yield curve and liquidity premium at τ and on the maturity and amortisation characteristics, including prepayment of the loan.

There is considerable expense associated with origination[3] due diligence, servicing the loan and in collections if the loan goes non-accrual or into delinquency. These direct (variable) expenses are a function of credit quality, whether directly originated or through a broker or dealer and the size of the loan. Direct expenses are computed through an activity-based costing and for a loan, usually expressed as a fraction of the balance:

$$Exp_{direct}(t) = \delta * B(t)$$

Traditional performance measures

Performance measurement is carried out over a period eg, a calendar month, quarter or a year. Let us consider performance of the loan for the calendar period $\tau + t$ to $\tau + t + 1$. One of the most common traditional performance measures is contribution margin (CM). Ex-ante, it is given by:

$$CM_{loan} = r_c(t) * B(t) + fee(t) - F_\tau * (1 - \lambda) * B(t) - Exp_{direct} - EL(t)$$

Ex-post, EL can be replaceed by actual $Loss$ in the period

$$CM_{loan} = r_c(t) * B(t) + fee(t) - F_\tau * (1 - \lambda) * B(t) - Exp_{direct} - Loss(t)$$

For example, we can look at the cash flows in the month of January 2006 from a five-year loan originated in April 2004.

The cash flows are contributed not only by the single loan in question but all performing loans in the portfolio in January 2006, of all different vintages. We define $\hat{B}$ as the total balance of all accruing loans of all vintages. The performance measure is, therefore, for a period across all different vintages. The subscript pf is used to denote a portfolio of loans:

$$CM_{pf} = \sum_{all\_loans}^{all\_vintages} CM_{loan}$$

$$NI_{pf} = (1 - tax\_rate) * [CM_{pf} - Exp_{overhead}]$$

$$ROA_{pf} = \frac{NI_{pf}}{\sum_{all\_loans}^{all\_vintages} B(t)}$$

It is easy to extend the above measures to a business unit, which may have revenues and expenses from other products which are not credit products (eg, retail deposits). One traditional performance measure, return on (book) equity, that can only be defined at the business unit level is:

$$ROBookE_{bus\_unit} = \frac{NI_{bus\_unit}}{\sum_{all\_loans}^{all\_vintages} [Assets(t) - Liabilities(t)]}$$

There are a couple of traditional measures which are related to portfolio credit only (and not revenues or expenses) and have been used for credit businesses for decades. These are non-performing loans ratio abbreviated as *NPL*, and net charge-off ratio abbreviated as *NCO*:

$$NPL\_Ratio = \frac{\sum\limits_{all\_vintages} B(t)_{non\_perf}}{\hat{B}}$$

In the numerator of the above formula, the balance of a non-performing loan is the balance after some part of the outstanding balance at default has been charged off in accordance with general accounting rules or prevalent practice in the financial institution. *NPL* is usually expressed as a percentage or in basis points. *NCO*, defined below, is generally expressed in basis points:

$$NCO = \frac{\sum\limits_{all\_vintages} B(t)_{charged\_off}}{\hat{B}}$$

Risk-adjusted performance measures

The traditional performance measures are clearly not altogether devoid of risk. Interest rate risk is captured by *FTP* and some part of credit risk captured by *EL*. Both *FTP* and *EL* are parts of traditional performance measures. What is meant by risk-adjusted performance measure is that it takes into account *all* risks, including unexpected (but not catastrophic) credit risk and operational risk. As has been described in Chapter 3, the single currency in which all such risks are captured is *economic capital*. As it so happens, the risk-adjusted measures that will be discussed also tie up with shareholder value creation.

For some years, heads of financial institutions have paid a lot of attention to its stock price or market capitalisation but have managed on a month to month basis using traditional performance measures. The latter will always remain important but in recent years, there has been a significant amount of emphasis placed on non-traditional performance measures. The stock price is affected by many factors on which neither the corporate manager nor the business unit manager has any influence. Therefore, particularly for the business units, it is necessary to have a measure that is, by and large, directly influenced by the business unit managers and at the same time is strongly correlated with shareholder value creation. Stern Stewart's EVA is one such measure. It has been shown that EVA has by far the strongest correlation with market value creation than any other profitability measure like EPS, NI, ROE or ROA. This is true for financial companies as well as industrial companies (see Uyemura, 1997 and Uyemura *et al*, 1996 for details).

The shareholder value creation imperative has received attention in financial institutions somewhat later than it did in many industrial organisations. Banks have introduced performance measures similar to EVA such as SVA, EP or EPA with a view to enhance shareholder value creation. Other banks have introduced ratio measures such as RORAC or RAROC.

The *EP*, simply incorporates a charge for capital to the traditional measure:

$$EP_{pf} = NI_{pf} - k * EC_{pf}$$

where k is the required rate of return per dollar of economic capital. The required rate of return is the same for all products and business units in the financial institution, since all risks in the product are captured in the economic capital attributed to it (discussed in Chapter 3). One common method of obtaining k is to use the CAPM as follows:

$$k = r_f + \beta * [E(r_M) - r_f]$$

where r_f is the risk-free rate and $E(r_M)$ is the expected return of a broad market index like the S&P 500 Index and β is the well-known measure of systematic risk of the company (financial institution).

A ratio measure that is a counterpart of *EP* is *RORAC*:

$$RORAC_{pf} = \frac{NI_{pf}}{EC_{pf}}$$

If *RORAC* ≥ *k*, *EP* ≥ 0 and vice-versa.

Pricing of a credit product

The pricing of a loan consists of setting the coupon (whether floating or fixed) to be charged and fees to be collected, such that the bank is compensated for the financial risk taken in adding the loan to its portfolio. In the sections and sub-sections above, we have considered the cash flows and performance measures over a period. But for purposes of pricing, it is necessary to take into account the *life-time* cash flows expected from the product. Note that here the summation is not across vintages but across time over the life of the loan. Taking all risks into account, the life-time economic profit from a loan (an ex-ante measure) is given by:

$$
\begin{aligned}
Lifetime\_EP_{loan} = \sum_{t=1}^{T} \frac{1}{(1+k)^t} [r_c(t) * B(t) + fee(t) - F_\tau * B(t) \\
- Exp_{direct}(t) - EL(t) - k * EC(t)]
\end{aligned}
$$

Equivalently, one can also define a ratio life-time ex-ante measure:

$$
RORAC_{loan} = \frac{\displaystyle\sum_{t=1}^{T} \frac{1}{(1+k)^t} [r_c(t) * B(t) + fee(t) - F_\tau * B(t) - Exp_{direct}(t) - EL(t)]}{\displaystyle\sum_{t=1}^{T} \frac{1}{(1+k)^t} * EC(t)}
$$

Note that the discount rate is the same as the required rate of return per unit economic capital. It can be shown that *only when* the discount rate is k, one can preserve the familiar relationship between the two life-time measures, that is: if $RORAC \geq k$, $Lifetime\_EP \geq 0$ and vice-versa.

It is important to understand the implications of the distinction between: (a) performance measures over a short period $\tau + t$ to $\tau + t + 1$ across all vintages τ; and (b) performance measures over the product lifetime for a particular vintage τ. First of all, in any period, they are not likely to be similar, let alone the same. Yet such divergence causes considerable misgivings for those used to traditional financial accounting.

It is not uncommon for banks to tighten credit underwriting at the beginning of and through a recession. It is also associated with charging higher price for credit even though demand may be soft.

This results in low origination or new production but at a better risk-adjusted return. At the same time, the existing portfolio is deteriorating leading to higher economic capital, higher NPL and NCO. The life-time risk-adjusted performance measures for new production are higher than or near normal while the single-period risk-adjusted performance measures for the portfolio are (much) lower than normal. This, usually baffling, divergence of the two types of performance measures at times of credit cycle downturn is at the root of many a misunderstanding when non-traditional performance measures are introduced for the first time at such a downturn.

Another source of much confusion among finance professionals is also related to the credit cycle. At the downturn, the credit deterioration of the portfolio increases the economic capital. No doubt the defaulted loans consume a lot of economic capital. But the loans which have deteriorated but not defaulted (in regulatory terminology, criticised and classified loans) are much larger in number and overall consume more economic capital in dollar terms. Most of these loans recover as the credit cycle improves and the economic capital drops several times. During this credit cycle, these loans are still in accrual status and do not impact traditional performance measures like CM_{pf} or NI_{pf} significantly. However, the performance measures like EP_{pf} or $RORAC_{pf}$ go through huge fluctuations as the credit cycle first deteriorates and then improves again. In percentage terms, such fluctuations can be just as much as fluctuations in NPL or NCO as the credit cycle moves through the trough. The latter is not surprising, nor should the former.

Other credit products

In this section so far, performance measures have been defined, both *ex-ante* and *ex-post*, with specific reference to a loan as a credit product. This has been done to provide clarity in preference to generality. For other credit products, the measures used are *the same* but their components are somewhat different. For a loan, coupon payment is one major component of CM or NI and so is FTP. For a customer derivative, neither of these is a component.

To provide one illustration of other credit products, let us consider a *line of credit* (an off balance sheet item) with maturity T. Let $L(0)$ be the line at origination and let $L(t)$ be the unused portion at time t for $t = 1$ to T. The average utilisation, u_{avg} of the line of credit is given by:

$$u_{avg} = \frac{1}{T} \sum_{t=1}^{T} \frac{L(0) - L(t)}{L(0)}$$

and is usually expressed as a percentage. The utilisation towards default, u_{def} reflects the amount of the line that an obligor is expected to draw down on its way to default. u_{def} is a somewhat different concept from u_{avg}. First, u_{def} is generally much larger than u_{avg}. Second, the higher the credit quality, generally lower is u_{avg} but higher is u_{def}. This is because a highly rated company generally has an approved line which is so high than under normal circumstances, it does not draw even 20% of the line. But when it is in hard times, the line of credit can be drawn down rapidly, usually with very little monitoring and without breaking any covenant. u_{def} can be as high as 80%.

The expected loss for the line of credit is given by

$$EL(t) = u_{def} * L(t) * PD * LGD$$

where $ex\text{-}ante\ EAD(0) = u_{def} * L(0)$ is an estimate. The line of credit is considered as part of a portfolio of other senior loans and lines. The economic capital attributable to the credit risk in the line as part of a portfolio of loans and lines is dependent on the correlation of default amongst the loans in the portfolio as well as on the probability of default and loss given default. The function $G[\ldots]$ is non-linear in general:

$$EC_{credit}(t) = u_{def} * L(t) * G[PD, LGD, Correlation]$$

A line, just like a loan, typically would have operational risk[4] which can be also measured in the same "currency" namely economic capital and we can write:

$$EC(t) = EC_{credit}(t) + EC_{operational}$$

As before, let us consider performance of the line of credit for the calendar period $\tau + t$ to $\tau + t + 1$.

$$CM_{LOC} = fee * L(t) - Exp_{direct} - EL(t)$$

Ex-post, we can replace EL by actual $Loss$ in the period

$$CM_{LOC} = fee * L(t) - Exp_{direct} - Loss(t)$$

Another common traditional measure is:

$$NI_{LOC} = (1 - tax\_rate) * [CM_{LOC} - Exp_{overhead}]$$

where $Exp_{overhead}$ is the business unit's overhead allocated to the line of credit.

The use of the above performance measures for a line of credit to a highly rated (say Fortune 500) company, has led to considerable pain and one-time charges by many financial institutions during the last two recessions in the USA. During normal and good years of the credit cycle, the utilisation of a LOC to the company is very low. While the fee is proportional to the size of the LOC, the drawn amount is negligible and actual loss zero. Thus larger the size of the LOC, the higher is CM_{LOC} and NI_{LOC}, even if the fee is just a few basis points. The larger the size of the LOC, the better it is for the borrowing company not only cosmetically but also from the perspective of risk. The financial institution also uses the size of the LOC as a good-faith gesture to obtain investment banking or cash management business from the company. As a result, the size of the LOC has little to do with the actual need of a line by the company. The performance in terms of traditional measure during normal and good years of the credit cycle is good though not spectacular.

But when one such company gets into financial difficulty, usually at the downturn of the credit cycle, it draws on the LOC in a matter of days. The financial institution has very little monitoring and built-in covenants to prevent such draws – hence u_{def} is very high sometimes nearing 100%. The loss to the financial institution is huge, much larger than was ever contemplated at the time of negotiating the size of the LOC.

Unlike the traditional measures, the non-traditional risk-adjusted performance measure picks up the effect. The economic capital is computed using u_{def} not u_{avg}. In the case of a highly rated company, u_{def} can be a order of magnitude higher than u_{avg}. As a result, with a few basis points of fee, the economic profit is likely to be negative:

$$EP_{LOC} = NI_{LOC} - k * EC_{LOC}$$

The ex-ante performance measures for purposes of *pricing* are very similar to those derived for a loan:

$$Lifetime\_EP_{LOC} = \sum_{t=1}^{T} \frac{1}{(1+k)^t}[fee * L(t) + \{r_c(t) - F_\tau\} * u_{avg} * L(0)$$
$$-Exp_{direct} - EL(t) - k * EC(t)]$$

or equivalently:

$$RORAC_{LOC}$$
$$= \frac{\sum_{t=1}^{T} \frac{1}{(1+k)^t}[fee * L(t) + \{r_c(t) - F_\tau\} * u_{avg} * L(0) - Exp_{direct} - EL(t)]}{\sum_{t=1}^{T} \frac{1}{(1+k)^t} * EC(t)}$$

PRICING AND PERFORMANCE OF A CREDIT-BASED RELATIONSHIP

Most financial institutions have become providers of multiple kinds of financial products well beyond an intermediary for borrowing deposits and lending to companies and consumers. These include money management, cash management, foreign exchange transaction on behalf of a client, offering of interest rate derivatives, mergers and acquisition advice and a plethora of loan and deposit products. It is rare for a customer (whether a firm or a consumer) to have only one product with a bank. The relationship usually consists of more than one product. Huge investments in customer relationship management (CRM) systems have facilitated financial institutions to create productive "relationships" with their customers. The return on such investments is generally suspect but that only escalates the importance of appropriately measuring customer or relationship profitability.

Relationship profitability measures are fundamentally similar to product profitability measures and can be both ex-ante and ex-post. In either case, the revenues, expenses, cost of funds (if any), expected losses and economic capital resulting from all products contained within the relationship have to be taken account of. Often the main credit product is a "loss leader" and has a negative economic profit or a *RORAC* less than the required rate of return on capital k. The other products may be *actually in place or potential ones* in the case of ex-ante relationship performance measures and are *actual products* used by the customer in case of ex-post relationship performance measures. All the components of the performance measures are additive (from product to product leading to the relationship) except for economic capital. It is not uncommon to assume that across the products that constitute a relationship, economic capital is additive.[5]

Therefore, the two common ex-post or realised performance measures can be expressed as:

$$CM_{relationship} = \sum_{relationship}^{all\_products} CM_{products}$$

$$EP_{relationship} = \sum_{relationship}^{all\_products} EP_{products}$$

and the corresponding ex-ante risk-adjusted performance measure used for pricing individual products being offered can be expressed as:

$$Exp\_EP_{relationship} = \sum_{relationship}^{all\_products} \sum_{all\_scenarios} Prob(scenario) * EP_{product}(scenario)$$

It is pertinent to mention that however rigorous the computation of funds transfer pricing, economic capital and expense allocation, the estimation of *Prob(scenario)* is generally very crude and undependable. Business unit managers tend to systematically over-estimate *Prob(Scenario)* for most optimistic scenarios and therefore, by definition, under-estimate *Prob(Scenario)* for pessimistic scenarios.

---

1   A typical instalment loan will fully amortise the balance at maturity so that $B(T) = 0$. But there are many instances of commercial loans in which the amortisation schedule is longer than the maturity T. In this case $B(T)$ is still 0 but there is a significant bullet payment between $T - 1$ and T. The notations are general enough to cover all such amortisation characteristics.

2   The operational risk for a loan is relatively small compared with credit risk and even interest rate risk. Interest rate risk, however, is managed by treasury and accounted for by funds transfer pricing rather than by economic capital.

3   Credit underwriting may or may not be a direct expense. In some institutions, it is an overhead expense.

4   The operational risk for a loan is relatively small compared with credit risk and even interest rate risk. Interest rate risk, however, is managed by Treasury and accounted for by funds transfer pricing rather than by economic capital.

5   This is strictly not correct since the institution is a multi-product business and can leverage off the diversification that different products provide. But it can be argued that each of the products could have been a stand-alone business (competing with mono-lines) and must provide return on a stand-alone basis.

REFERENCES

Basel Committee on Banking Supervision, 2001, "The New Basel Capital Accord", Consultative Document, January (CP2).

Basel Committee on Banking Supervision, 2003, "The New Basel Capital Accord", Consultative Document, April (CP3).

Canabarro, E., E. Picoult, and T. Wilde, 2003, "Analysing Counterparty Risk", *Risk*, **16(9)**, pp 117–22.

Gordy, M., 2003, "A Risk-Factor Model Foundation for Ratings-Based Bank Capital Rules", *Journal of Financial Intermediation*, **12(3)**, pp 199–232.

Gordy, M. and D. Jones, 2003, "Random Tranches", *Risk*, **16**, pp 78–83.

Merton, R., 1974, "On the Pricing of Corporate Debts: the Risk Structure of Interest Rates", *Journal of Finance*, **29**, pp 49–70.

Pykhtin, M. and A. Dev, 2002, "Credit Risk in Asset Securitisations: Analytical Model", *Risk*, May, pp S16–S20.

Pykhtin, M. and A. Dev, 2003a, "Coarse-grained CDOs", *Risk*, January, pp 113–16.

Pykhtin, M. and A. Dev, 2003b, "Residual Risk in Auto Leases," Risk, October, pp S10–S16.

Uyemura, D. G., 1997, EVA: A Top-down Approach to Risk Management, *Journal of Lending and Credit Risk Management*, **79(6)**, p 40.

Uyemura, D. G., C. C. Cantor, and J. M. Pettit, 1996, EVA for Banks: Value Creation, Risk Management and Profitability Measurement, *Journal of Applied Corporate Finance*, **9(2)**, pp 94–113.

Vasicek, O., 1987, *Probability of Loss on Loan Portfolio*, Washington DC: KMV Corporation.

Vasicek, O., 1991, *Limiting Loan Loss Probability Distribution*, Washington DC: KMV Corporation.

7

Improving Risk-Adjusted Performance through Active Credit Portfolio Management

INTRODUCTION

Historically, banks have originated wholesale loans and held them until they matured or defaulted. In recent years with the advent of active credit portfolio management (ACPM) and the development of capital market instruments like credit default swaps, basket default swaps, commercial mortgage backed securities, synthetic collateralised debt obligations, collateralised loan obligations, the situation has changed for corporate credit portfolios in large institutions as well as commercial real estate financing. However, for portfolios consisting of exposures to small and medium enterprises (SME), almost all banks are still in the "originate and hold" mode.

Since the concept of ACPM in traditional banking is quite new and yet relatively complex, most readers may not be familiar with it and may be asking the question: what is ACPM? In the next section, therefore, we introduce ACPM in a general way. Since there are very few capital market credit instruments that directly tie to SME credits, readers may conclude that ACPM is not for SME portfolios. To address this aspect, we have specifically addressed ACPM for SME credits in a separate section, with examples of strategies.

ACPM's main objective is reaching a more efficient risk/return profile and thus enhancing overall risk-adjusted performance of the financial institution. We provide a possible strategy for optimising or at least enhancing portfolio risk-adjusted return for all credits in general and SME portfolios in particular.

In another section, we introduce the concept of credit transfer pricing (CTP). ACPM generally requires a separation between portfolio management from loan origination & relationship management. As the difference in objectives of these two activities creates friction, even to the point of bringing ACPM decision making to a halt, it is necessary to create an economic separation between portfolio management and loan origination. This can best be achieved through a transfer-pricing mechanism. We provide a mechanism of CTP using economic capital as the basis that is economically fair.

Finally, we provide a detailed derivation of risk-adjusted performance measure(s) for the ACPM function. By focusing on this measure(s), the overall risk-adjusted performance of the financial institution can be significantly enhanced.

ACPM INTRODUCED

Portfolio management is not a new concept. It is used extensively in managing equity and bond investments. At the core of portfolio management are Markowitz's (mean-variance) portfolio diversification principle and Sharpe's capital asset pricing model (CAPM).[1] However, this concept has not been widely used by bankers managing loan portfolios in general and middle market portfolios in particular. Traditionally bank loan portfolios have been characterised by:

❑ origination by stand-alone transaction analysis;
❑ "originate and hold" strategy;
❑ client relationship focus; and
❑ volume based performance metrics for originators.

Also, traditionally, while a portfolio view is taken to set concentration limits and for strategic decisions, a formalised tactical function of portfolio management has not been setup.

The following developments in the last eight to ten years have made it feasible to look beyond the traditional approach:

❑ considerable liquidity in the secondary market for bank loans;
❑ quantitative modelling of credit risk;
❑ a measure of portfolio diversification benefits (knowledge of correlations);

❏ an EC framework and ability to measure risk adjusted returns; and

❏ development of credit derivatives markets.

The underwriting or rating process looks at the risk characteristics of an individual transaction. This process can be compared to that of a bricklayer cementing individual bricks while constructing a wall. Standing next to the wall, the additional brick lays in perfectly. But it is necessary to stand back a certain distance and view whether the wall, as a whole, is going up straight or not. This view of the wall as a whole is the portfolio approach. In every discussion between the originating (sales) authority and the credit approval authority, the overall view of the wall needs to be kept in mind.

The activities and analytics of credit portfolio management can be viewed to cover a whole spectrum. At one end of the spectrum is a pure transaction view of facilitating the origination of credit risk to customers. At the other end of the spectrum is a prescriptive view (concentration limits, industries caps, etc) of limiting the accumulation of credit risk. Between these two ends lies a wide opportunity of portfolio (optimal) decision-making – with a strong reliance on quantitative analysis. A few years ago, *Risk* magazine carried a story on how a few banks were preparing themselves for a paradigm shift in management of portfolio credit risk, where analytics played a central role (Risk 2002). The skill sets required for ACPM are also quite different from the skill sets of many traditional credit underwriters and lenders (Reidy 2005).

ACPM also necessarily creates a separation between portfolio management on the one hand and loan origination and maintenance of a relationship on the other. The objectives of the two may very well be different. This separation is best achieved through a transfer pricing mechanism. Later in the chapter, we will show how an economically fair credit transfer pricing mechanism can be built on the framework of EC.

Recently the International Association of Credit Portfolio Managers[2] (IACPM) has published a list of sound practices for staffing and managing the ACPM function in a financial institution. The sound practices have been grouped under descriptive headings with the following themes (please see IACPM (2005) for more details):

❑ Define the portfolio to be managed.
❑ Identify the role and mandate of the CPM function.
❑ Standardise risk measures and models.
❑ Deal with data issues.
❑ Understand economic value versus accounting value.
❑ Set limits and manage concentrations.
❑ Stress test the portfolio.
❑ Align accounting conventions with portfolio management practices.
❑ Rebalance the portfolio to achieve strategic objectives.
❑ Establish objectives and measure performance.
❑ Be transparent in disclosures.

Although addressed primarily for ACPM for large corporate portfolios, the sound practices are, by and large, sound business practices and are also applicable to ACPM of SME portfolios.

Since ACPM was initially developed to improve the financial performance of the large corporate loan portfolio, the IACPM document tends to focus on more liquid credit markets and emphasises trading activities that are available in these markets. However, for mid-sized banks with SME portfolios, volume is not likely to be enough to set up a market-making trading function. ACPM function may be content with obtaining market quotes from dealers. ACPM is, in principle, all about reducing portfolio credit risk. It is not about making trading and profits. Mixing these two objectives in a bank is poor judgement, at best. We believe that the objective of ACPM in the less liquid credit markets is not to make trading profits, but to reduce portfolio risk and enhance overall risk-adjusted returns.

Figure 1 is a schematic diagram of an integrated framework for ACPM. The framework of ACPM consists of a holistic view of portfolio credit risk. It includes active feedback from a portfolio perspective to the underwriting process, a perspective that the field credit and sales personnel do not have. This reverse feedback loop, which is just as important as taking positions in capital market credit instruments for SME portfolios, is often overlooked in discussions on ACPM.

From an ACPM perspective, analytics and strategy matter much more than efficiency of execution of a trade or sale in the capital markets. In asset management, (model-driven) asset allocation

Figure 1 A typical ACPM framework

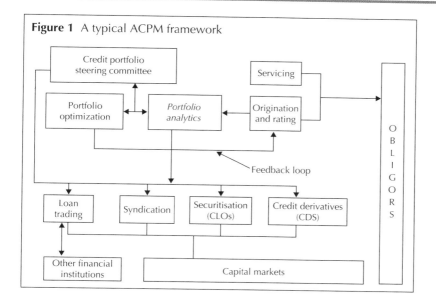

strategy matters much more than security selection; this, in turn, matters much more than market timing (efficiency of execution), insofar as portfolio performance attribution is concerned.[3] In exactly the same way, sector selection is far more important than name selection, which in turn is far more important than trading efficiency in determining the effectiveness of ACPM.

ACPM FOR SME CREDITS

The private companies that constitute the borrowers of a SME portfolio typically do not have publicly traded equity or bonds. These loans are rated internally by the bank. Capital market investors are not familiar with the companies whose liabilities constitute the underlying collateral and naturally demand large amounts of excess collateralisation and higher coupons. On the other hand, these investors are conscious of the element of diversification in a pool of middle market or small business loans. We have little doubt that liquid capital markets will develop for transactions of middle market credits sooner or later. It will probably take several years. In the meantime occasional deals are being done,[4] perhaps to test the waters. But the more important question is whether banks with predominantly SME portfolios have to stay away from ACPM.

A typical SME portfolio does not have the single-name loan concentrations to a small set of companies that dominate the horizon as "tall trees". But institutions holding predominantly SME loans on their books are often:

❏ concentrated in a few geographies/sectors; or
❏ exposed to companies falling within a relatively small number of industries/sectors.
❏ The obligors themselves do not have cash flows coming from diversified sources and activities.
❏ There is a preponderance of commercial real estate lending within limited geographies.
❏ There is consumer (residential or otherwise) lending to individuals dependent on the health of the very same sectors and geographies.

These characteristics of SME loan portfolios result in significant concentrations of credit risk when the economy of a particular geography experiences an economic contraction or a particular industry loses its competitive position. An obvious example is lending to automobile manufacturing companies (although they are not strictly SMEs) and their suppliers and funding real estate of automobile dealers in the mid-west of the US.

Our concept of ACPM also includes another aspect which is useful to those pricing unrated loans. The prices, spreads and discounts and their changes observed in the capital markets can be used as benchmarks or signals for a sanity check on the pricing in the field. This is not to say that the margin on the middle market loans in a particular sector should be calibrated to say, average bond spreads in that sector. The size of a small business loan relative to overheads alone will make such a calibration meaningless.

It is pertinent to note the central role played by portfolio analytics in this framework. The importance of this central role of portfolio analytics in ACPM cannot be overemphasised since market discipline of no-arbitrage pricing cannot be relied upon for SME exposures. In the absence of broad, deep markets, portfolio managers of SME credit risk relies heavily on analytical models to guide their decision making.[5] What might come as a surprise to many readers is that the relative importance of analytics is more in

ACPM of SME portfolios than in ACPM of large corporate loan portfolios.

Very few SME names trade in the credit default swap market. Nor are there industry-specific indices trading in the CDS market. CLOs of SME loans are frequently uneconomical and often do not transfer economic risk. This is because (a) the underlying loans may be under-priced; (b) investors require a premium for buying CLO tranches with underlying collateral that is unfamiliar (as yet) to them; (c) the issuing bank has to hold a first loss piece which is usually in excess of reasonable EC to support the whole of the underlying portfolio.[6] The selling of whole or part of a performing loan in a relatively illiquid SME loan trading market comes with a significant discount. To a lender, as long as the loan is performing well (no credit event) selling such a loan at a significant discount is anathema.

What is a bank with predominantly SME exposures to do, if it wishes to hedge part of its portfolio credit risk? One way is to buy CDS on rated names in sectors in which the SME portfolio has too much exposure. For example, if the SME portfolio consists of too much exposure to commercial real estate (CRE), then taking long position(s) in CDS on REIT(s) invested partly in the same geography can provide a hedge, though imperfect. However, in a typical SME portfolio, even if one sector may hog a significant portion of the portfolio size, there is considerable intra-portfolio diversification within the sector. That is, within a SME portfolio, there are numerous obligors or projects within each sector and none is large enough. Consequently the idiosyncratic risk within each sector has been diversified away, resulting in an effectively higher sensitivity to correlation between (cumulative) exposure in one sector and that in another sector (for a formal proof see Pykhtin 2004). The effect of ACPM strategies by leveraging inter-sector correlations (of systematic factors) is actually stronger, in proportional terms, for SME exposures than for large corporate exposures with "tall trees". This is a subtle but important point that motivates the need for ACPM of SME portfolios.

Hedging with credit default swaps has a recurring cost but no significant up-front cost. The buyer pays a spread (CDS spread) in return for the credit protection. In case of default (or restructuring in some cases) the seller of protection pays the notional to the buyer and assumes the defaulted bond. Thus the SME bank effectively reduces its net interest margin (NIM) on that part or all of the asset by hedging (equal to the notional of the CDS). This cost is offset by reduction in economic and regulatory capital. Depending on the market and the extent of concentration in the portfolio, this may or may not add to shareholder value.

A material difficulty for taking long positions in CDS is the accounting treatment. Under most structures, the hedge (long position in CDS) has to be MTM.[7] The loan is recorded at historical cost, with credit loss provisioning while the hedge must be recorded at fair value. CDS spreads are volatile and may show significant movement even when there is no perceptible credit event as hedge-funds and some other investors move in and out of CDS positions based on considerations not necessarily connected with credit.

In single name CDS on companies rated triple B+ or below, a large move (200 to 500 bps) in spread over a short period is not improbable.[8] The following is an extreme (but still not improbable) example to illustrate how the outcome of the position in single name CDS can have a significant effect on SME banks' earnings and will depend very much on management's risk appetite. Consider a 5-year single-name CDS of US$350 million notional at a spread of 700 bps. Suppose that the CDS spread tightens by 500 bps and then widens by 500 bps in the other direction in a month or two.[9] The MTM effect of each of the events (tightening/widening) on this position would be approximately US$50 million, in two different directions. To put some perspective of the MTM effect on SME banks' earnings, consider an SME bank with assets of US$50 billion and return on assets (ROA) of 1.2%. The MTM effect of US$50 million represents the whole month pro-rated net income, or one-third of the quarterly earnings. For the SME bank with a long position, a MTM loss upon tightening of the CDS spread will completely wipe out that month's net income or equivalently, reduce the quarterly *eps* by one third.[10] Given the pre-occupation of CFOs of banks (or for that matter any company, except the ones which are most innovative) with stable *eps* and meeting analysts' consensus forecast, this scenario will be considered disastrous.[11] The SME bank's risk management[12] would be in a panic mode since they are not used to extreme volatility in P/L resulting from large trading positions. It is likely that stop-loss conditions would be imposed and the position would be unwound immediately. The bank would end up with a loss of US$50 million or so. If the bank did hold on (very unlikely) to the position even after booking the huge loss, it would not have had to report any loss at all in the quarter concerned. The example above has been shown simply to ring a cautionary note.

A bank can finance the purchase of protection (long in single name CDS) by selling protection (short in a single name CDS) in another sector in which the SME portfolio is light. The spread income received from the short position compensates for the net interest margin or earnings reduction from the hedge. At the same time, the risk of significant MTM hit from spread volatility is partially mitigated. If the MTM hit in the hedge results from economy-wide credit deterioration or improvement (eg, in 2000–1 there was a systemic increase in CDS spreads and then in 2003–4 there was a systemic decrease),[13] then the long and the short positions are likely to move in opposite directions, muting the magnitude of the MTM effect.

There is a positive side to selling protection all on its own. The SME bank creates exposures to companies (most likely of higher credit quality than most SME exposures) with which the bank does not have any relationship nor does it presume to create one. If the bank's credit underwriters can assess the credit risk of an unrated SME, there is no reason to doubt that they will be able to rate a public company, which is already highly rated by the rating agencies and on which plenty of public information is forthcoming. The short CDS exposures are in sectors that are likely to have low correlation with the rest of the SME portfolio exposures, because the sectors chosen are deliberately ones in which the SME portfolio is light. The overall portfolio credit risk after the long and short positions will very likely go down. More revenue is generated by the SME bank with less portfolio credit risk, thus enhancing overall RAROC. This brings us to the following section. Also, short CDS exposures are likely to be liquid, allowing entry and exit as desired, and do not involve relationship issues.

ENHANCING PORTFOLIO RISK ADJUSTED RETURN

Domestic credit risk is often correlated but the extent of correlation varies depending on many different characteristics. Second, the correlation is nowhere near 100%. Therefore, even if the exact values of these correlations are not known, it is easy to show that a higher efficiency frontier can be achieved simply by taking action from a portfolio perspective. By taking of a portfolio view and maximising risk-adjusted return by leveraging possible diversification effects is at the core of ACPM. The risk of a loan depends not only on the risk characteristics of the transaction, but also equally on how it correlates with the rest of the portfolio. It is necessary to take stock of the overall portfolio in terms of portfolio risk at regular intervals, excessive risk to be lightened up, additional names to diversify, etc. Holding reserves against individual transactions is not enough to mitigate or reduce credit risk that is unexpected in nature. This is where economic capital comes in.

Default correlation between an industry or sector and another is not easy to estimate since default is a rare event and data over long history are hard to come by. However, the correlation between the stock index for one sector and the stock index for another sector is observable and so are the volatilities (implied from option prices). A structural model like the well-known Merton–Vasicek framework (Merton 1974, Vasicek 2002) can then be used to derive default correlation. This may not be a reasonable approach to obtain default correlation (or equivalently asset value correlation) between one SME exposure and another. The option-theoretic framework of distance-to-default does not apply well to non-traded SME companies. The fundamental concepts of correlation and portfolio diversification are much more valid for SME portfolios. Only no one knows precisely what the values of the correlations are.

Even though it is difficult to pin down the precise values of correlations, a rank ordering can be done by most experienced lenders and credit risk managers. It is not too difficult to see that the fates of auto-part suppliers and automobile dealers go together (high correlation) while between steel manufacturers and software developers, default correlation will be low. Thus an n-dimensional matrix can be drawn up and each cell assigned one of five ordinal values: Very High (VH), High (H), Medium (M), Low (L) and Very Low (VL). The last one may even extend into negative correlation territory.

It is a much easier task to calculate a pair of numbers representing the percentage exposures (of total portfolio) to the corresponding pair of sectors that the cell represents in the matrix. These can then be entered as a pair of numbers in each cell. Alternatively, the numbers can be bucketed into categories very high (*vh%*), high (*h%*), medium (*m%*), low (*l%*), and very low (*vl%*). The resultant matrix is shown in Figure 2. Entries have been made to the matrix in Figure 2 purely as illustrations, where the entries in capitals letters refer to inter-sector correlation buckets and the entries in small italic letters refer to the sector's share (%) in the total exposure.

The third step is to identify cells that have the lowest correlation (VL), lowest share (*vl*) of one sector in the SME portfolio and the highest share (*vh*) of the other sector in the portfolio. The ideal cell will be something like VL (*vh,vl*) but such a cell may not exist. Even if it does, the third step is complete only when the best five or more (depending on the magnitude of the matrix) cells have been identified. The best we have in the illustrative Figure 2 is the cell corresponding to sectors S1 and S4. That is, S4 is a good candidate[14] for

Figure 2 ACPM strategy matrix

	S1	S2	S3	S4
S1	VH (*m%,m%*)	H (*m%,h%*)	H (*m%,vl%*)	VL (*m%,l%*)
S2	H (*h%,m%*)	VH (*h%,h%*)	M (*h%,vl%*)	M (*h%,l%*)
S3	H (*vl%,m%*)	M (*vl%,h%*)	VH (*vl%,vl%*)	VL (*vl%,l%*)
S4	VL (*l%,m%*)	M (*l%,h%*)	VL (*l%,vl%*)	VH (*l%,l%*)

the bank to take a short position in CDS on a traded name that represents sector S4 for expanding investment opportunity in the area where the bank is not active.

The fourth step is to select some names in each of the low share (*vl* or *l* preferably) sectors in the identified cells using the following criteria: (a) a group of experienced commercial lenders become comfortable with those names, (if necessary) after doing some fundamental analysis using publicly available information; (b) historical volatility of CDS spread and bond spread is relatively low; and (c) fairly liquid CDS which trades more or less every day. This would narrow down the possible single-name CDSs in which the bank may take a short position, ie, sell protection.

The fifth step is to find cells that have the highest correlation, highest shares of the two sectors in the SME portfolio. The one which is ideal will be something like VH (*vh,vh*) but such a cell may not exist. Even if it does, as before, the step is complete only when the best five or more (depending on the number of cells with *vh* and *h*) cells have been identified. The best we have in Figure 2 are those cells corresponding to sectors S1 and S2. That is, S1 and S2 seem good candidates for long CDS positions (hedging) for the bank.

The sixth step is to select some names in each of the high share (*vh* or *h*) sectors in the identified cells using the following criteria: (a) historical volatility of CDS spread and bond spread is relatively low; and (b) fairly liquid CDS which trades more or less every day. This would narrow down the possible single-name CDSs in which the bank may take a long position (ie, buy protection or hedge) or a short position (ie, sell protection).

At the end of all these steps, the results need to be presented in a coherent fashion in a ACPM *strategy*. The strategy document should include contingent scenarios of future net interest margins, possible MTM gains or losses and recalculated EC. The strategy we have enumerated is not terribly complex. A simple computer program can be written to do the first five steps. However, the sixth step requires the portfolio manager's knowledge and understanding of the institution's risk appetite, concern for cosmetic ratios of the institution and strategic plans in the near future, not to speak of dynamics of the private loan market and customer relationships. Thus, it must not be left to a program.

The ultimate financial and performance objective is to enhance RAROC or SVA, EVA or EP of the credit portfolio, subject to certain limits on other accounting and cosmetic ratios. Here as well as elsewhere in the bank, this is at the root of achieving a shareholder value creation paradigm. The matrix strategy suggested is obviously aimed at reducing EC and enhancing earnings. But even if there is small reduction of earnings let alone enhancement in earnings, there can be strategies of reduction in EC, by leveraging sector correlations, which justifies the ACPM strategy.

CREDIT TRANSFER PRICING

One of the secondary aspects of ACPM is a separation between portfolio management from loan origination and maintenance of a relationship. The objectives of the two functions may very well be different. This can lead to considerable friction, even bringing ACPM decision making to a halt in extreme cases. An economic separation between portfolio management and loan origination can be best achieved through a transfer pricing mechanism. In this section we will develop an economically fair credit transfer pricing mechanism built on the framework of economic capital. Further, we will show that through a transfer pricing mechanism, the possible conflict between the portfolio management and loan origination business units can be resolved.

The concept of transfer pricing in banking is somewhat different from the concept of transfer pricing in international finance. Transfer pricing of funds taking into account interest rate risk (abbreviated FTP) has been commonplace between treasury and business units in a bank for a number of years. Transfer pricing of credit (abbreviated CTP) is still in its infancy.

The FTP rate is the opportunity cost of money. The opportunity cost of money is easily observable from yield curves derived from highly liquid interest rate products. The cost of funds curve for a financial institution of a particular debt rating is usually a spread over the Treasury or libor-swap yield curve. All these are (liquid) market-clearing spreads, easily observable and readily available from a market source like Bloomberg.

FTP in a bank applies to *both* sides of the balance sheet. Corporate treasury charges an appropriate rate on every dollar outstanding of all assets and credits an appropriate rate on every dollar outstanding of all liabilities. For an asset and a liability with identical principal cash flows and prepayment characteristics, the rate charged for the asset is the same as the rate credited to the liability. The magnitude of net FTP cash-flows to the FTP offset centre is small in comparison with the sum of the FTP charges on the individual assets. Since a bank is highly leveraged (almost 20:1), most of the reduction in cumulative FTP charges results from netting charges on assets with credits on liabilities. Diversification of interest rate risk across assets of differing terms and amortisation is negligible.

CTP obviously applies to only *one* side (the asset side) of the balance sheet. Any reduction in cumulative CTP cash-flows can only result from diversification of credit risk across assets. In a credit portfolio this diversification is significant.[15] However, if the portfolio is nearly asymptotic ie, a very large number of transactions each of which is negligible in size in comparison with the portfolio size, then the marginal contribution to diversification of an additional transaction is also negligible.

The main objective of an FTP is to find out the contributions to net interest income made by each internal business unit or product or manager or by treasury. By analogy, we characterise the main objective of CTP as one of finding out the relative contributions to EP[16] (see Chapter 1 for definition of *EP*) or equivalently, pre-tax economic profit (*EBPT*) made by each internal business unit or product or manager or by credit portfolio management. EPBT is simply pre-tax earnings minus a pre-tax charge for EC.

In general EC is the economic capital required to support all the risks associated with a business unit or product. Since we are concerned with CTP in this chapter, we abstract from all other risk and consider EC as credit risk economic capital.[17] Note that, in accounting terminology, while EC is a stock variable, the pre-tax required return on equity, $(k / 1 - \tau) * EC$ is a flow variable. By its very definition, CTP must be a flow variable. Therefore, the expression above and the fact that the objective of CTP is to determine the relative contributions to pre-tax EP, suggests that $(k / 1 - \tau)$ may be a good candidate for the CTP rate charged for the per-unit credit risk. Here τ is the effective tax rate.

Another objective of FTP is to isolate the business units from future fluctuations in interest rates; effectively to transfer that risk to the Treasury function. By analogy, the objective of the CTP is to isolate the business units from uncertainty of how the future credit cycle will play out; in this case transfer that risk to the Portfolio Management (PM) function. While this may be possible in the case of institutional lending, it is a tall order for SME portfolios to transfer all credit risk to PM.

A CTP *rate* of $(k/1-\tau)$ implies that the CTP charge per unit of loan exposure does not depend on the characteristics of the loan; the total CTP cash-flow does depend on the credit characteristics as well as the size of the loan. This is in contrast with FTP, where not only the total FTP cash-flow but also the FTP *rate* itself depends on the term and amortisation of the individual asset or liability as well as its size. It is as if each asset is charged FTP on a stand-alone basis. In credit portfolios,[18] each loan cannot be charged CTP on a stand-alone basis because of the intra-portfolio correlation.

Let j represent sector. Let us consider the ith loan in the jth sector with outstanding balance of $b(i, j)$ which is considered funded by equity portion $ec(i, j)$ the economic capital attributed to the loan and debt portion defined by $d(i, j) = b(i, j) - ec(i, j)$. How much each individual loan should be funded by equity depends on the risk characteristics of the loan. The EC charged on the SME portfolio of the jth sector is $EC(j) = \Sigma_i ec(i, j)$.

Figure 3 below shows cash and fund flows among obligors, all units of the bank, debt holders, equity holders, and credit capital market dealers. Note that thick arrows indicate flows (typically one time) of stock variables and thin arrows flow variables (periodical flows).

The business unit j receives revenue from all SME customers i in the sector j. Each business unit is charged a fund transfer pricing, $FTP(j)$ by the treasury function, and a credit transfer pricing, $CTP(j)$ by the portfolio management (PM) function. The treasury pays a cash flow of $\overline{FTP}$ to the corporation, and the corporation in turn pays the interest due to debt holders. Since we are concerned with credit transfer pricing in this chapter, it is assumed that $\Sigma_j FTP(j) = \overline{FTP} =$ interest payments to debt holders.[19]

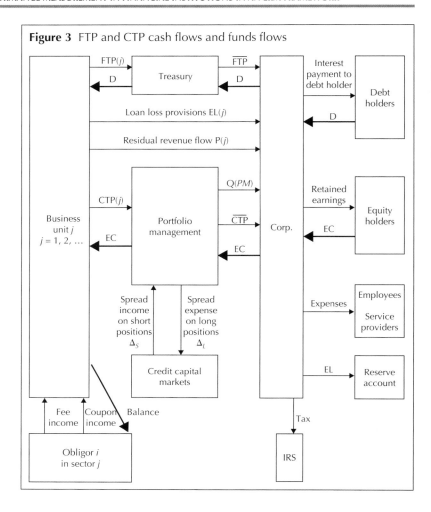

Figure 3 FTP and CTP cash flows and funds flows

Similarly, a simplified approach is taken to expenses since this chapter is concerned with credit transfer pricing. No distinction is made between direct expenses and overhead expenses. It is assumed that the total expenses are paid by the corporation to employees and vendors etc and allocated to the business units and portfolio management by some activity-based-costing mechanism. Note that total expenses sum to expenses allocated to all units:

$$Expenses = \sum_j Exp(j) + Exp(PM) + Exp(TRY)$$

The loan loss provision for each loan is assumed to be equal to the expected loss (EL). For a portfolio of loans, $\Sigma_j\Sigma_i EL(i, j) = \Sigma_j EL(j) = EL$. Actually the actions of the PM unit will have second order effects on resultant EL and the above relationship may not hold exactly. It is assumed that this effect is negligible or the difference is made up at the reserve account to which the loan loss provisions flow.

The CTP rate charged per unit of EC is $k/(1 - \tau)$, which does not depend on the characteristics of the loan. The CTP cash-flow charged by the PM to the business unit engaged in originating all loans in sector j will be

$$CTP(j) = \sum_i \frac{k}{1 - \tau} ec(i, j) = \frac{k}{1 - \tau} EC(j)$$

The residual revenue flow, $P(j)$ from business unit j to the corporation is given by:

$$P(j) = \sum_i [r_c(i, j)b(i, j) + fee(i, j) - EL(i, j)]$$

The corporation pays taxes to the authorities and the resultant retained earnings flow to the equity holders.

Portfolio Management may take both long and short positions in the credit capital markets.[20] To keep matters simple, only single-name CDS are considered as the credit instruments used by the PM. Let Δ_L and Δ_S be total payments of CDS long positions and total receipts of CDS short positions respectively.[21] Let ΔMTM be changes in the mark-to-market of all CDS positions.

Let E be the portfolio EC computed before any action is taken by the PM function, ie, $E = \Sigma_j EC(j)$. $\bar{E}$ is defined as the equivalent portfolio EC after positions have been taken by the PM function. The transfer pricing charge from the corporation to the portfolio management function is given by:

$$\overline{CTP} = \frac{k}{1 - \tau} \bar{E}$$

It is worth noting that the calculation of $\bar{E}$ as well as of E requires running a full-blown economic capital model. In the case of SME portfolios, there are large number of transactions, each individually small and we can use the asymptotic single risk-factor property (see Gordy 2004) to help us in attributing $EC(j)$ to each transaction in a simple way, thus making the otherwise inevitable discussions, transaction by transaction, on CTP charge between line managers and the PM function less onerous. However, it is believed that even if the parameters of the economic capital model are only approximate, most of the benefits of ACPM can still be derived.

PERFORMANCE MEASUREMENT OF ACPM

The net revenue flow, $Q(PM)$ from the PM function to the corporation is given by:

$$Q(PM) = [-\Delta_L + \Delta_S + \Delta MTM]$$

The net pre-tax economic profit of the portfolio management function is represented as $EPBT(PM)$ and its expression is given by.

$$EPBT(PM) = \frac{k}{1-\tau} E + Q(PM) - \frac{k}{1-\tau} \bar{E} - Exp(PM)$$

where $Exp(PM)$ is the expense allocated to the PM function. Note that if the PM does nothing (ie, not take any positions in CDSs), then $\bar{E} = E$ and $Q(PM) = 0$ by design. In that case $EBPT(PM) = -Exp(PM)$, just as in the case of any purely expense function like legal or audit in a financial institution. Rearranging terms in the $EBPT(PM)$ expression,

$$EPBT(PM) = \frac{k}{1-\tau} [E - \bar{E}] - [-Q(PM) + Exp(PM)]$$

The EP (risk-adjusted performance measure introduced in Chapter 1) contributed by ACPM is:

$$EP(ACPM) = k * [E - \bar{E}] - (1 - \tau) * [-Q(PM) + Exp(PM)]$$

The term $[E - \bar{E}]$ is clearly the portfolio economic capital *reduction* achieved by the portfolio management function. The first term in the above expression can, therefore, be interpreted as the *benefit* added by the PM function (to which the business units have no claim). The second term within brackets can be interpreted as the *cost* (in terms of cash flow) of achieving the economic capital reduction.[22]

Changes in the MTM in CDS positions in the expression for the revenue and thus in the expression for $EP(ACPM)$ has some serious implications since CDS spreads are volatile and may show significant movements over a short period (see the section on ACPM for SME Credits for examples). Over some quarters, changes in the MTM in CDS positions may dominate all other items in $EP(ACPM)$ even if $\bar{E}$ is significantly less than E. In the initial period of setting up the ACPM function in a bank, it may not be judicious to include it when measuring the performance of the PM function over a short period, especially since the objective of ACPM is not to make trading profit or losses but to reduce portfolio credit risk and enhance overall risk-adjusted returns over a long period. This does not mean that the MTM gains/losses are ignored. They are facts of life in a business world subject to accounting rules. They are certainly going to show up in the corporation's income statements. But at this juncture, when it comes to internal performance, MTM gains/losses will likely be absorbed by the corporation – where short-term fluctuations in the MTM value of, say, the CDS book will still be small in comparison with the overall quarterly net income and also there will be some diversification effects.

This suggestion is not as unorthodox as it appears. For several decades, internal performance measurement for business units in most financial institutions have been based on contribution margin, which ignores several items below the line being absorbed by the corporation. Therefore, excluding changes in the MTM in CDS positions may be more meaningful performance measure:

$$Perf(ACPM) = k * [E - \bar{E}] - (1 - \tau) * [\Delta_L - \Delta_S + Exp(PM)]$$

An efficient PM function can be expected to keep $Exp(PM)$ low and strategically choose sectors and positions (notional amounts) of CDS, so that cds_L and cds_S are not that far apart while $\bar{E}$ is significantly less than E. The point to realise is that this is achieved through portfolio analytics and optimisation, taking the current CDS market as given and not through trading skills. Depending on the market spreads and the initial portfolio composition, the value of the term $Perf(ACPM)$ can be significantly positive. The overall *performance* of the financial institution, measured in terms of EP, can thus be *enhanced significantly* through ACPM. Equivalently, the ratio risk-adjusted performance measures like RORAC can be enhanced significantly. For example, an increase from a percentage of low tens to a percentage of high tens will be a huge enhancement in a competitive environment.

CONCLUSION

Active credit portfolio management (ACPM) is a development of the last 10 years, where the basic ideas of equity/bond portfolio management are applied to commercial loans. Traditionally banks have been lending to commercial firms with an "originate and hold" mind-frame. That mode is by and large true even today of SME portfolios. The obligors in these portfolios are typically private companies with neither bonds nor publicly traded equity.

Many large banks are already active in ACPM for their institutional credit portfolios. There are very few capital market credit instruments that directly tie to SME credits. Does that mean banks with predominantly SME portfolios should stay out of ACPM for the time being? The answer is "no", but they need to understand the risks involved and the potential benefits to the bank's short-term performance. They may venture out of their "originate and hold" mode but they cannot afford to negatively affect their relationship focus, however fancy ACPM may sound.

In a typical SME portfolio, the exposures are limited to a relatively small number of sectors (industries, geographical regions etc). A single sector may hog a significant portion of the portfolio size. However, there is considerable *intra-portfolio* diversification within the sector. That is, within an SME portfolio, there are numerous obligors or projects within each sector and none is large enough. Consequently the idiosyncratic risk within each sector has been diversified away, resulting in an effectively higher sensitivity to correlation between (cumulative) exposure in one sector and that in another sector. The effect of ACPM strategies by leveraging *inter-sector* correlations (of systematic factors) is actually *stronger*, in proportional terms, for SME exposures than for large corporate exposures with "tall trees". We argue that this somewhat surprising concept provides a theoretical motivation for ACPM for SME portfolios.

In this chapter, we also introduce a credit transfer pricing (CTP) mechanism that is economically fair to all the parties and serves two major objectives: (1) to learn the relative contributions to pre-tax economic profit made by each internal origination unit or product or manager and also by credit portfolio management; and (2) to create a separation between the portfolio management and loan origination through which the possible conflict between the portfolio management and loan origination units can be resolved. The methodology proposed is based on EC and therefore presupposes the availability of an EC model for portfolio credit risk and credit risk in capital market products. However, even if the EC model is only approximate, most of the benefits of ACPM can still be derived.

ACPM's main objective is reaching a more efficient risk/return profile and thus enhancing overall risk-adjusted performance of the financial institution. We provide a possible strategy for optimizing or at least enhancing portfolio risk-adjusted return for all credits in general and SME portfolios in particular. A risk-adjusted performance measure(s) for the ACPM function is introduced and derived in details. The higher this measure(s), the higher will be the overall risk-adjusted performance of the financial institution.

1   See Smithson and Hayt (2000–2001).
2   IACPM was formed in 2001 and has played a yeoman's role in bringing together ACPM practitioners and in disseminating knowledge about portfolio credit risk, capital market credit instruments and ACPM.
3   Commercial bankers and credit risk managers are surprisingly unaware of this fact and of performance attribution in asset management in general. Therefore, there is a danger of spending too much effort in committees about specific names and timing of trade, etc, and too little effort on sector selection and analytically driven strategy proposals.
4   Issuance of middle market CLOs in the USA, (though still relatively small) increased by 36% from 2004 to 2005. See LPC Gold Sheets, *Middle Market*, **XII(12)**, December 2005. But it is already clear that 2005 will be "a tough act to follow". See LPC Gold Sheets, *Middle Market*, **XX(7)**, February 2006.
5   Credit portfolio managers in broad, deep markets also rely heavily on analytical models, but the existence of liquidity enables these portfolio managers to achieve much greater precision in their efforts to maximise long-term returns on these positions.
6   Banks in Europe are selling 100% of the first loss positions in SME CLOs.
7   A few particular structures of CDS have received accrual treatment in the past but in view of the current regulatory (accounting or otherwise) environment, the accounting treatment is likely to be all MTM.
8   For example, CDS spread on Ford tightened by almost 200 bps during the month of October 2002, and widened by almost 300 bps within a period of 30 days in March–April 2005. During the period of 2001 to 2002, many corporate credits were downgraded and CDS spreads of those so called "fallen angels" jumped over short periods.

9 As an example, consider the case of AEP during the period of October and November 2002. The CDS spread went from 350 bps to 950 bps and then came back to 300 bps. At times, such volatility is not even driven by signs of credit deterioration or improvement.

10 In reality, this example overstates the MTM effect to the extent that the bank is likely to hedge exposure to various entities so that there would be the portfolio effect on MTM of CDSs. On the other hand, the total notional on a variety of names can be several times the US$350 mm example. For a US$50 billion SME bank, a portfolio of CDSs with total notional of US$1 billion is conceivable. On a long-only CDS portfolio of US$1 billion notional, even with portfolio effect, it is possible to wipe out more than a month's earnings.

11 Analysts like stable earnings. The accounting mismatch between loans and derivative hedges introduces significant P&L volatility. The FASB is entertaining comments on a fair value option that would allow loans to be accounted for at fair value.

12 Traders, however, will be thrilled with this volatility because their bonuses are asymmetric and by and large contemporaneous, ie, they get paid handsomely on the upside but the institution suffers the downside.

13 Fitch Ratings (2004) reported systemic increase in CDS spreads peaking in the summer of 2002 and subsequent systemic decline till year-end 2003. Fitch Ratings (2005) again reported a systemic decrease in CDS spreads in 2004.

14 Note that at first sight, S3 and S4 seem good candidates for the bank to take short CDS positions. Taking a short CDS position in S3, however, can exacerbate risk exposure to S1 (because of high correlation between S1 and S3), and thus, S3 is not a good candidate for the short position in CDS.

15 McQuown (2003) reports that a UK bank was able to triple its originations to large corporations without altering its capital base as a direct consequence of improved diversification. As the portfolio manager constantly rebalances the portfolio to maintain the performance of economic capital, line managers do not have to worry about concentration of the origination of business in one area.

16 Variants of EP are Economic Value Added (EVA) and Shareholder Value Added (SVA).

17 EC for credit consists of two components: default only and marked-to-market (MTM). For simplicity only EC is considered as default.

18 Not just in SME portfolios but in all credit portfolios, the effect of correlations will always make CTP different from FTP in this regard.

19 In practice, Treasury will manage IRR by taking positions in interest rate swaps and high quality investment instruments and issue debt at a few appropriate times of the year. Since we are focusing on credit transfer pricing, we elect to abstract from the complexity resulting from such activities.

20 In the first chapter in this series, it has been explained with illustrations how this strategy helps both in reducing MTM hits as well as minimizing reduction in current earnings.

21 The expressions for the total cash flows from long and short CDS positions are:

$$\Delta_L = \sum_j \sum_m cds_{L,j}(m)N_{L,j}(m) \qquad \Delta_S = \sum_j \sum_m cds_{S,j}(n)N_{S,j}(n)$$

where $N_{L,j}(m)$ is the notional of the mth long position, $N_{S,j}(n)$ the notional of the nth short position, $cds_{L,j}(m)$ the CDS spread of the mth long position, and $cds_{S,j}(n)$ that of the nth short position in the sector j.

$$\Delta MTM = \sum_j \sum_m \Delta MTM(j,m) + \sum_j \sum_n \Delta MTM(j,n)$$

where $\Delta MTM(j, m)$ is the change in market value of the mth long position in sector j and $\Delta MTM(j, n)$ is the nth short position in sector j.

22 $Q(PM)$ can be positive or negative. But the way it has been defined it is a net *revenue*. $-Q(PM)$, therefore, is a *cost*.

REFERENCES

Ferry, J., 2002, "New Players, New Rules," *Risk*, May.

Fitch Ratings, 2004, "Global Credit Derivatives Survey: Single-Name CDS Fuel Growth," Special report on Credit Policy, September.

Fitch Ratings, 2005, "Global Credit Derivatives Survey: Risk Dispersion Accelerates," Special report on Credit Policy, November.

Gordy, M.B., 2004, "A Risk-Factor Model Foundation for Ratings-Based Bank Capital Rules," in A. Dev (ed), Economic Capital: A Practitioner Guide, Risk Books.

Guill, G., 2005, "Credit Portfolio Management: An Introduction to the Challenges and Opportunities of this emerging field," *The RMA Journal*, July/August.

IACPM, 2005, 'Sound Practices in Credit Portfolio Management," IACPM website, http://www.iacpm.org/reference_articles/, November.

IACPM, 2005, "Middle-market Vendor Default Model Study," unpublished working paper, July.

Loan Pricing Corporation Gold Sheets, 2005, *Middle Market*, **XII(12)**, December.

Loan Pricing Corporation Gold Sheets, 2006, *Middle Market*, **XX(7)**, February.

Merton, R., 1974, "On the Pricing of Corporate Debt: The Risk Structure of Interest Rates," *Journal of Finance*, **29**, pp 449–470.

Pykhtin, M., 2004, "Multi-factor Adjustment," *Risk*, March, pp 85–90.

Reidy, P. E., 2005, "Corporate Credit Portfolio Management: Changing Skills Requirements," *The RMA Journal*, July/August.

Smithson, C. and G. Hayt, 2000–2001, "Managing Credit Portfolios by Maximizing Risk-Adjusted Return," *The RMA Journal*, December–January.

Vasicek, O., 2002, "Loan Portfolio Value," *Risk*, December, pp 160–162.

8

Modelling and Measuring Performance of Indeterminate Deposits

INTRODUCTION

Non-maturity or indeterminate deposits are customer deposits in a bank with no contractual maturity date. Together with contractual time deposits or certificate of deposits, they form what are known as "core" deposits. Indeterminate deposits are numerous transaction level accounts with small (generally) outstanding balances and with daily transactions. For traditional retail and commercial banks, a large proportion of revenue and earnings is attributable to spread and fee income from non-maturity deposits. Therefore, measuring the performance of non-maturity deposits appropriately and consistently is imperative for such banks. The lack of a predetermined cash-flow pattern (hence the term "indeterminate") and the administered nature of how the product rates are arrived at make it a very difficult task to measure, let alone predict, performance of non-maturity deposits accurately. A formal modelling approach is called for.

For purposes of FTP and interest rate risk, the non-maturity deposits are modelled not at the account or transaction level but at the product category level. The typical product categories are as follows: *interest checking, savings, demand deposits* (usually separated into those belonging to personal, business and public bodies), *money market* and *indexed products*. The non-maturity deposits exhibit *three* characteristics that require special modelling considerations. First, they have *no contractual* maturity or amortisation schedule. Second, some of them have *product rates* that are set *administratively*. Third, in some of the products, the customer can earn a *reduction in fee* even though no interest is paid.

PROJECTION METHODOLOGY

Typically monthly data are available of both deposit balances for each product category and for the product rate charged. The end of month (EOM) balances show much more fluctuation than do average daily balances (ADBs). The ADBs show a marked pattern over the months. It is difficult to find such a pattern in the EOM balances.

Deposits are modelled in the following way: balances are assumed to follow a time-related pattern. Growing balances grow at a decreasing rate over time, while decaying balances decay at a slower rate over time. This is built into the functional form of the regression. A logical reason for time decay comes from the fact that, over the period in question, customers are becoming more sophisticated, both in terms of money management information and in terms of efficiency in transactions. Information about the opportunities for investing in mutual funds and other investments with higher returns (some even providing the transactions facilities that demand deposits have traditionally provided) has proliferated. Customers, however, have a wide spectrum of information and propensity to move their money into alternative investments and do not act homogeneously. As a result balances fall slowly over time. Deposit balances are also adjusted for seasonality.

For each product category, the balance is projected into the future using the available monthly data for all the *previous months*. The time trends (or "lines of best fit") are actually non-linear. The best fit for each product category is obtained by using *regression* analysis. The actual data points are scattered around the best fit. The errors or deviations from the trend are computed and their standard deviation calculated. At any point in time, the predicted or expected balance minus 3 standard deviations is considered the minimum value the balance can have, in all probability. Of course, the balance always has a chance of going below this level, but it is highly unlikely.

CORE AND NON-CORE

The *core* component of the balance is defined as the *projected balance* minus 3 standard deviations. The *non-core* balance is defined as the realised balance (ADB) minus core balance. Since the realised

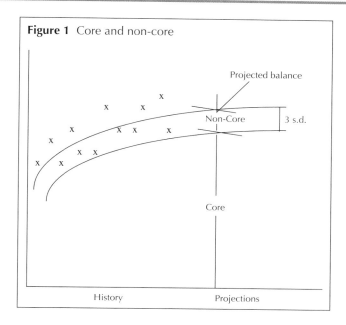

Figure 1 Core and non-core

balance is not likely to fall below the core because 3 standard deviations are subtracted from the projected balances to arrive at the core, the non-core is almost always positive. The non-core balance for any month drops off in the next month (the non-core principal amortises in one month).

Figure 1 illustrates how the core and non-core components are determined. The x's represent actual ADBs observed.

The balances used to arrive at core and non-core are *net* of floats and reserves.

Treatment of the Core

The schedule for the core balances (the schedules are consistent with each other) to be used depends on the application. Table 1 gives the details.

In the economic valuation, the "close the books and go home" philosophy has been adopted.

Treatment of the non-core

❑ Non-core balances are treated as short (1 month) money for all applications;

❏ current month non-core is the current balance minus the (pro-jected) core in the current month;

❏ projected non-core is essentially the seasonal predictions plus the 3 Std Dev component; and

❏ non-core is rate dependent. Rate sensitivity based on analysis of national data.

Table 1 Schedule for core balances

Application	Schedule used	Remarks
Funds transfer pricing	Vintage schedule	Going forward
	Portfolio runoff schedule as well as vintage schedules	Starting point
GAP analysis	Portfolio runoff schedule	Directly
Earnings forecast	Fungible dollar growth/decay	
Economic valuation	Fungible dollar growth/decay	Under "going concern" philosophy
	Portfolio runoff schedule	Under "close the books and go home" philosophy
Liquidity (business as usual)	Fungible dollar growth/decay	
Liquidity (crisis)	Portfolio runoff schedule suitably adjusted	

Table 2 Schedules for different applications

Application	Schedule used	Remarks
Funds Transfer Pricing	One month money	
GAP analysis	One month cash flow	Directly
Earnings forecast	Fungible dollar growth/decay	With rate dependence
Economic valuation	One month cash flow	Under "going concern" philosophy
	One month cash flow	Under "close the books and go home" philosophy
Liquidity (business as usual)	Fungible dollar growth/decay	
Liquidity (crisis)	Runoff in one month	

A FEW REMAINING CONCEPTS IN THE MODEL

One of the purposes and benefits of modelling indeterminate deposits is that it ensures that FTP and all balance sheet risk analysis are based on a consistent set of assumptions. The schedules created during the modelling process are automatically made consistent with observations at the macro level as well as the new production volumes. The three different schedules or trends introduced below are self-consistent. The fact that they are used in different applications does not mean the applications are inconsistent.

Vintage schedule

This is the amortisation schedule for the core balance of a given vintage. The vintage schedule is the same for every month of issuance. Obviously, vintage schedule different for different product categories.

Portfolio runoff schedule

The portfolio schedule is derived from vintage schedules and using information about the total (over all vintages) core balance projected for a particular month.

Fungible dollar decay or growth

Historical trend (non-linear decay or growth) of balances — looked upon as a fungible dollar amount (irrespective of transaction or vintage) — over time. This implies that lagged balances are independent variables but not lagged interest rates. The functional form will obviously be different for different product categories. The rate dependence of the trend is only for large changes in interest rates.

Product rate (for administered rate products)

Product rate changes for administered rate product groups should be modelled as a function of a benchmark rate that the pricing committees pay attention to. The benchmark rate can be the Federal funds target rate or the 3-month libor rate or the Donahue index rate. It is recommended that the modeller restricts to one benchmark rate only. In a rising (falling) rate environment, product rates are ratcheted up (down) in a stepwise fashion. The magnitude of the change is, in all cases, a fraction of the benchmark rate movement. Product rates are generally modelled as being more responsive to falling (benchmark) rates than to rising rates. Product rate increases occur with a greater lag than rate decreases. The increases also tend to occur in larger increments. Convexity is, therefore, built into the response function. The three features of the product rate modelling are:

❑ asymmetric product rate changes in response to interest rate changes (positive or negative);
❑ product rate responding to interest rate changes with a time lag; and
❑ product rate responding to interest rate changes, only if the change is large.

Market value
The market value of the non-maturity deposit as a liability is calculated as the present value of cash paid out of the bank. Cash flows out of the bank in a month consist of the principal drop from month to month, the interest expense (which may be zero) and the non-interest expense in a month.

Economic value
The economic value of the non-maturity deposit to the bank is the par value minus the market value.

DEMAND DEPOSIT PRODUCTS
DDA products are transaction accounts, which are paid a *product rate* of *zero*. Customers of DDA products can obtain a reduction in fees by maintaining a certain balance. The fees are typically floating rate (T-bill rate). Thus these balances are effectively paid the short rate, even though the product rate is, by definition, zero. It is assumed that a certain percentage of the core balance for each product category belong to customers that carefully manage their money and obtain the floating rate. Thus the core is divided into floating core and fixed core. The following are illustrative floating core percentages:

DDA business	30%
DDA personal	10%
DDA public bodies	20%

The assumed lives or amortisation schedule for a particular vintage is the same for fixed and floating core. The floating core, however, gets the short rate (which is variable as time progresses) plus a liquidity premium. The fixed core gets a weighted average rate based on the amortisation schedule (which remains fixed over time) for the given vintage.

Vintage schedules

The amortisation schedules for core deposit balances are typically near exponential. Thus, runoff in near-term months is faster than runoff in more distant months. The following tables provide (purely illustrative) principal drops based on the exponential vintage schedule, at various time intervals:

For business DDA, the principal drop at various time intervals is:

	Principal drop after (%)
1 month	0.8
12 months	9.0
24 months	18.0
60 months	38.0
120 months	58.0

For DDA personal, the principal drop at various time intervals is:

	Principal drop after (%)
1 month	0.65
12 months	8.0
24 months	15.0
60 months	32.0
120 months	54.0

For DDA public bodies, the principal drop at various time intervals is:

	Principal drop after (%)
1 month	0.37
12 months	4.0
24 months	8.5
60 months	20.0
120 months	35.0

Portfolio schedules

First we need to create the portfolio at month T_0. The portfolio schedules are derived from vintage schedules using information about the total (over all vintages) core balance projected for a particular month. The starting point is T_0. The core balance at T_0 is formed out of vintages for the prior 120 months. The vintages to be considered (ie, having something left over at T_0) go backwards all the way to month $T_0 - 120$, because the schedule for core deposits extends 10 years.

Since the vintage schedules are known, starting from an unknown $x(t)$ dollar amount created as each month's vintage, we can obtain the core balance available at T_0, as a function of $x(t)$ ($t = 1, 2,\ldots,120$) where $x(t)$ grows or diminishes with t according to the same non-linear time trend used to project balances. We can then solve for $x(t)$, as we know the actual Core balance prevailing at T_0. Once the unknowns $x(t)$ ($t = 1, 2, \ldots, 120$) have been obtained, the portfolio schedule for the core balance T_0 is known.

Now we can create the portfolio going forward (creation of new core). The balance that is scheduled to drop off in the month $T_0 + 1$ from the portfolio as a whole is known. The remaining core balance from the T_0 portfolio is thus known. The projected balance minus 3 standard deviations, on the other hand, gives the core balance in month $T_0 + 1$. By subtracting the former from the latter, the new core created in the month $T_0 + 1$ is obtained. This new core then starts to amortise according to the vintage amortising schedule. This process is repeated for every month up to the current month.

Vintage specific FTP rates

The rate environment corresponding to a particular vintage (month) consists of:

(1) a base cost of funds term structure, which is the monthly average of the (mid-point of the bid-ask spread) daily libor-swap Curves – converted to monthly compounding; and
(2) a liquidity premium term structure schedule.

A single FTP rate for each vintage is arrived at from (1) the term structure(s) above; and (2) the vintage amortisation schedule. The

Appendix provides detailed methodology (mathematical expressions) as to how the vintage specific FTP rates, viz the vintage specific Base rate and vintage specific liquidity premium, are arrived at.

Overall FTP rate

At any month, any remaining balance of the fixed core, created at a particular vintage, carries the vintage specific Base rate and the vintage specific liquidity premium. At any month, the total fixed core consists of fixed core created at different vintages. The fixed core base rate (liquidity premium) is the weighted average rate of the vintage specific base rates (liquidity premia). The *FTP rate* for the *fixed core* at any month is the *weighted average base rate plus the weighted average liquidity premium.*

At any month, any remaining balance of the floating core, created at a particular vintage, carries the vintage specific liquidity premium. At any month, the total floating core consists of a floating core created at different vintages. The floating core liquidity premium is the weighted-average rate of the vintage specific liquidity premia. The *FTP rate* for the *floating core* at any month is the *short (1-month) rate plus the weighted-average liquidity premium.* The base rate is floating from month to month and does not carry any effect of vintage yield curves.

(1) The *non-core* gets the *short (1-month) rate*, which varies from month to month.
(2) The *overall FTP rate* is the weighted average of the fixed core FTP rate, floating core FTP rate and the non-core FTP rate.

Interest rate risk measurement

(1) The portfolio amortisation schedule is used to amortise the current fixed core balance for purposes of calculation of economic value, duration and convexity.
(2) The floating core and the non-core are run off in one month for purposes of calculation of economic value, duration and convexity.
(3) For purposes of earnings and earnings at risk, the portfolio amortisation schedule is not used to run off the balances. Instead the projected balances are used.

Table 3 Business DDA

(in US$bils.)	2005	2006	2007	2008	2009	2010	2011	2012	2013
Actual Balance	5.10	5.26	5.28	5.48	5.64				
Proj Balance	5.16	5.30	5.43	5.57	5.70	5.84	5.97	6.10	6.24
3 Std Dev	0.27	0.27	0.28	0.29	0.30	0.30	0.31	0.32	0.32
Core Balance	4.90	5.02	5.15	5.28	5.41	5.53	5.66	5.79	5.91

AN ILLUSTRATION

Tables 3 to 8 show an illustration of the methodology. The actual numbers are for illustrative purposes only and do not represent the characteristics of any particular bank. The example pertains to DDA business (core runoff exponential over 10 years) but the runoff every year is shown rather than every month. This allows one to illustrate the methodology with a limited set of numbers. The *annual time step* is *only* for the purposes of the following illustration at Tables 3 to 8. Actual implementation may use *monthly time steps*.

The illustration has so many numbers that the interested reader is advised to take a pencil and paper and do the step by step calculations, confirming the results with the numbers in each successive table. Alternatively, an excel spreadsheet can be set up to do the step by step calculations. The steps of the methodology are difficult to see at a cursory glance.

Table 3 shows the result of a hypothetical projection from past balances in order to derive a core and a non-core.

ADMINISTERED RATE PRODUCTS

The modelling of non-maturity deposits that have a product rate (or rate paid to the customer) which is administered can be done very similarly to that of demand deposit (including the illustrative example). The only difference is that the response of the product rate to market rate changes needs to be modelled explicitly. Typically such administered product rate setting is done somewhat separately in different regions of the financial institution's footprint. These rate settings often take the primary competitors' product rates into account and sometimes deliberately set it, say, somewhere near the median range of competitors' rates in the region, quite independently of the market rate. Thus it is usually

Table 4 Core amortising schedule for business DDA (2005 portfolio: unknown vintage amounts)

Vintage created in		Principal drop in									
		2006	2007	2008	2009	2010	2011	2012	2013	2014	2015
1996	1.00x	0.42 · 1.00x									
1997	1.04x	0.04 · 1.04x	0.42 · 1.04x								
1998	1.08x	0.05 · 1.08x	0.04 · 1.08x	0.42 · 1.08x							
1999	1.12x	0.05 · 1.12x	0.05 · 1.12x	0.04 · 1.12x	0.42 · 1.12x						
2000	1.15x	0.06 · 1.15x	0.05 · 1.15x	0.05 · 1.15x	0.04 · 1.15x	0.42 · 1.15x					
2001	1.19x	0.06 · 1.19x	0.06 · 1.19x	0.05 · 1.19x	0.05 · 1.19x	0.04 · 1.19x	0.42 · 1.19x				
2002	1.23x	0.07 · 1.23x	0.06 · 1.23x	0.06 · 1.23x	0.05 · 1.23x	0.05 · 1.23x	0.04 · 1.23x	0.42 · 1.23x			
2003	1.26x	0.08 · 1.26x	0.07 · 1.26x	0.06 · 1.26x	0.06 · 1.26x	0.05 · 1.26x	0.05 · 1.26x	0.04 · 1.26x	0.42 · 1.26x		
2004	1.30x	0.08 · 1.30x	0.08 · 1.30x	0.07 · 1.30x	0.06 · 1.30x	0.06 · 1.30x	0.05 · 1.30x	0.05 · 1.30x	0.04 · 1.30x	0.42 · 1.30x	
2005	1.33x	0.09 · 1.33x	0.08 · 1.33x	0.08 · 1.33x	0.07 · 1.33x	0.06 · 1.33x	0.06 · 1.33x	0.05 · 1.33x	0.05 · 1.33x	0.04 · 1.33x	0.42 · 1.33x
Total principal drop	8.10x	1 · 12x	1 · 04x	0 · 96x	0 · 88x	0 · 82x	0 · 76x	0 · 70x	0 · 65x	0 · 61x	0 · 57x

Equate 8.10x to the Core in 2005. x = US$0.60 billion.

135

Table 5 Core amortising schedule for business DDA (2005 portfolio: calculated vintage amounts)

Vintage created in		Principal drop in									
		2006	2007	2008	2009	2010	2011	2012	2013	2014	2015
1996	0.60	0.26									
1997	0.63	0.03	0.27								
1998	0.65	0.03	0.03	0.28							
1999	0.67	0.03	0.03	0.03	0.29						
2000	0.70	0.04	0.04	0.03	0.03	0.30					
2001	0.72	0.04	0.04	0.04	0.03	0.03	0.31				
2002	0.74	0.05	0.05	0.04	0.04	0.03	0.03	0.31			
2003	0.76	0.06	0.05	0.05	0.04	0.04	0.04	0.03	0.32		
2004	0.78	0.06	0.06	0.05	0.05	0.04	0.04	0.04	0.03	0.33	
2005	0.81	0.07	0.07	0.06	0.05	0.05	0.05	0.04	0.04	0.03	0.34
Total principal drop	4.90	0.68	0.63	0.58	0.53	0.49	0.46	0.42	0.39	0.37	0.34

Table 6 Core amortising schedule for business DDA (2006 portfolio including new core created in 2006)

Vintage created in		Principal drop in									
		2007	2008	2009	2010	2011	2012	2013	2014	2015	2016
1997	0.63	0.29									
1998	0.65	0.03	0.30								
1999	0.67	0.03	0.03	0.32							
2000	0.70	0.04	0.04	0.03	0.33						
2001	0.72	0.04	0.04	0.04	0.03	0.34					
2002	0.74	0.05	0.05	0.04	0.04	0.03	0.35				
2003	0.76	0.06	0.05	0.05	0.04	0.04	0.04	0.36			
2004	0.78	0.06	0.06	0.05	0.05	0.04	0.04	0.04	0.37		
2005	0.81	0.07	0.07	0.06	0.05	0.05	0.05	0.04	0.04	0.38	
New core created											
2006	0.81	0.08	0.07	0.07	0.06	0.05	0.05	0.05	0.04	0.04	0.38
Total principal drop	5.53	0.77	0.71	0.65	0.60	0.56	0.52	0.48	0.45	0.41	0.38

Table 7 Core amortising schedule for business DDA (2007 portfolio including new core created in 2006 and 2007)

Vintage created in		Principal drop in									
		2008	2009	2010	2011	2012	2013	2014	2015	2016	2017
1998	0.65	0.33									
1999	0.67	0.03	0.35								
2000	0.70	0.04	0.04	0.36							
2001	0.72	0.04	0.04	0.04	0.37						
2002	0.74	0.05	0.05	0.04	0.04	0.38					
2003	0.76	0.06	0.05	0.05	0.04	0.04	0.39				
2004	0.78	0.06	0.06	0.05	0.05	0.04	0.04	0.40			
2005	0.81	0.07	0.07	0.06	0.05	0.05	0.05	0.04	0.41		
New core created											
2006	0.81	0.08	0.07	0.07	0.06	0.05	0.05	0.05	0.04	0.41	
2007	0.83	0.09	0.08	0.08	0.07	0.06	0.06	0.05	0.05	0.04	0.42
Total principal drop	6.23	0.87	0.80	0.74	0.68	0.63	0.58	0.54	0.50	0.46	0.42

Table 8 Core amortising schedule for business DDA (2000 portfolio including new core created in 2006–2010)

Vintage created in		Principal drop in									
		2001	2002	2003	2004	2005	2006	2007	2008	2009	2010
2001	0.72	0.49									
2002	0.74	0.05	0.51								
2003	0.76	0.06	0.05	0.52							
2004	0.78	0.06	0.06	0.05	0.54						
2005	0.81	0.07	0.07	0.06	0.05	0.55					
New core created											
2006	0.81	0.08	0.07	0.07	0.06	0.05	0.55				
2007	0.83	0.09	0.08	0.08	0.07	0.06	0.06	0.56			
2008	0.85	0.10	0.09	0.08	0.08	0.07	0.06	0.06	0.58		
2009	0.87	0.12	0.10	0.10	0.09	0.08	0.07	0.06	0.06	0.59	
2010	0.89	0.13	0.12	0.11	0.10	0.09	0.08	0.07	0.07	0.06	0.61
Total principal drop	8.90	1.26	1.15	1.06	0.98	0.90	0.82	0.76	0.70	0.65	0.61

very difficult to data mine for patterns other than very simple pattern(s) that hold on average over a long period. To keep matters manageable, it is recommended that modelling be done with only one benchmark rate.

Product rate

Product rate changes for the administered rate product groups can be modelled as a function of a benchmark (market observed) rate eg the Federal funds target rate. In a rising (falling) rate environment, product rates are ratcheted up (down) in a stepwise fashion. The magnitude of the change is, in all cases, a fraction of the Federal funds rate movement. Product rates are modelled as being more responsive to falling Federal funds rates than to rising rates. Product rate increases occur with a greater lag than rate decreases. The increases also tend to occur in larger increments. Convexity is, therefore, built into the response function.

Table 9 shows illustrative product rate responses to various Federal funds rate change scenarios for an administered non-maturity deposit category. The table lists 25 possible rate change scenarios for the next 12 months and the corresponding responses given to each scenario.

Table 9 Product rate response assumptions

Scenario			Product rate change (bps)	In month
Rates up	300 bps in 12 months	then unchanged		
Rates up	275 bps in 11 months	then unchanged		
Rates up	250 bps in 10 months	then unchanged		
Rates up	225 bps in 9 months	then unchanged		
Rates up	200 bps in 8 months	then unchanged	10	8
Rates up	175 bps in 7 months	then unchanged		
Rates up	150 bps in 6 months	then unchanged		
Rates up	125 bps in 5 months	then unchanged		
Rates up	100 bps in 4 months	then unchanged		
Rates up	75 bps in 3 months	then unchanged		
Rates up	50 bps in 2 months	then unchanged		
Rates up	25 bps in 1 months	then unchanged		
Rates unchanged				
Rates down	25 bps in 1 months	then unchanged	−5	2
Rates down	50 bps in 2 months	then unchanged	−5	4
Rates down	75 bps in 3 months	then unchanged	−5	6
Rates down	100 bps in 4 months	then unchanged	−5	8
Rates down	125 bps in 5 months	then unchanged	−5	10
Rates down	150 bps in 6 months	then unchanged	−5	12
Rates down	175 bps in 7 months	then unchanged		
Rates down	200 bps in 8 months	then unchanged		
Rates down	225 bps in 9 months	then unchanged		
Rates down	250 bps in 10 months	then unchanged		
Rates down	275 bps in 11 months	then unchanged		
Rates down	300 bps in 12 months	then unchanged		

APPENDIX

Mathematics behind vintage specific FTP rate calculation

We associate an interest rate called the vintage rate with each new vintage coming in. Let the new core vintage in year 2000 be P (US$0.89 billion in our illustration). Let the current (say June 2006) yield curve be known and $r1$ represent the annually compounded one-year rate, $r2$ annually compounded two-year rate, etc. The vintage falls off $p1\%$ in the first year, $p2\%$ in the second year, and so on. That is, $p1\%$ of P will stay for 1 year, $p2\%$ for 2 years, and so on. In our example the cash flows due to interest are:

The total cash flow amount in the vintage's life time is

Year 1:	$0.09\,P \cdot R_1 \; + 0.08\,P \cdot R_2 \; + 0.08\,P \cdot R_3 \; + 0.07\,P \cdot R_4 \; \dots \; + 0.42\,P \cdot R_{10}$
Year 2:	$0.08\,P \cdot R_2 \; + 0.08\,P \cdot R_3 \; + 0.07\,P \cdot R_4 \; \dots \; + 0.42\,P \cdot R_{10}$
Year 3:	$0.08\,P \cdot R_3 \; + 0.07\,P \cdot R_4 \; \dots \; + 0.42\,P \cdot R_{10}$
Year 4:	$0.07\,P \cdot R_4 \; \dots \; + 0.42\,P \cdot R_{10}$
.	
.	
.	
Year 10:	$0.42\,P \cdot R_{10}$

$$CF = 0.09P \cdot R_1 \cdot 1 + 0.08P \cdot R_2 \cdot 2 + 0.08P \cdot R_3 \cdot 3$$
$$+ 0.07P \cdot R_4 \cdot 4 + 0.06P \cdot R_5 \cdot 5$$
$$+ 0.06P \cdot R_6 \cdot 6 + 0.05P \cdot R_7 \cdot 7 + 0.05P \cdot R_8 \cdot 8$$
$$+ 0.04P \cdot R_9 \cdot 9 + 0.42P \cdot R_{10} \cdot 10$$

A vintage rate f can be defined to be a single interest rate applied to the vintage such that the total cash flow is the same as above, ie,

$$0.09P \cdot f \cdot 1 + 0.08P \cdot f \cdot 2 + 0.08P \cdot f \cdot 3 + 0.07P \cdot f \cdot 4 + 0.06P \cdot f \cdot 5$$
$$+ 0.06P \cdot f \cdot 6 + 0.05P \cdot f \cdot 7 + 0.05P \cdot f \cdot 8$$
$$+ 0.04P \cdot f \cdot 9 + 0.42P \cdot f \cdot 10 = CF$$

Or in general, $f = \sum_t [P_t \cdot t \cdot R_t] / \sum_t [P_t \cdot t]$

This is the vintage rate associated with the core created in 2000. Similarly, given the core falling off schedule and the yield curve for a particular year, the vintage rate for that year can be calculated. Note that the vintage rate only depends on the core amortisation schedule, not on the actual amount of core coming in.

A step-by-step illustrative calculation of the cost of funds

(1) The FTP cost of funds consists of the base FTP rate and the liquidity premium.
(2) The raw market information that goes into the base FTP rate is the daily libor swap yield curve. The daily rates are averaged for the month, as FTP for non-maturity deposits is applied once a month on average monthly balances. The averaging process fills in the rates for weekends and holidays, using the rates for the last working day. The rate used from the quoted yield curve(s) is the mid-point of the bid-ask spread.
(3) Since non-maturity deposits are paid interest (if at all) computed monthly, the base FTP rate to be applied is the rate corresponding to monthly coupons. The term points of the yield curve up to one year are quoted as money market rates while the longer-term points are quoted as semi-annual coupon payments. All points of the yield curve are converted to rates corresponding to monthly coupons.
(4) The liquidity premium is dependent on the credit rating of the bank. While base FTP rates are computed every month, using daily observations, the liquidity premium is revised every quarter, unless special market conditions require major changes. The liquidity premium is zero up to 12 months.

The floating core amortisation schedules are *identical* to the fixed core amortisation schedules.

Table A1 An example of base cost of funds curve

Libor swap yield curve			Interpolated base COF	
Term	Quoted rates	Monthly compounded Rates	Term	
1 mo.	6.63	6.63	1 mo.	6.63
3 mo.	6.75	6.60	1 yr.	6.89
6 mo.	6.95	6.76	2 yr.	6.82
12 mo.	7.11	6.89	3 yr.	6.83
2 yr.	7.05	6.82	4 yr.	6.84
3 yr.	7.06	6.83	5 yr.	6.85
5 yr.	7.09	6.85	6 yr.	6.86
7 yr.	7.12	6.88	7 yr.	6.88
10 yr.	7.14	6.90	8 yr.	6.89
30 yr.	7.16	6.92	9 yr.	6.89
			10 yr.	6.90

Table A2 Base cost of funds curves for various vintages (1996–2006)

Base FTP rate for various vintages

Term	Principal drop	1996	1997	1998	1999	2000	2001	2002	2003	2004	2005	2006
1mo.		7.69	4.69	3.31	3.25	6.00	5.69	5.50	5.72	5.06	5.82	6.63
1 yr.	0.09	7.31	4.23	3.99	3.75	7.49	5.30	5.64	5.81	4.98	6.31	6.89
2 yr.	0.08	7.39	4.89	4.73	4.31	7.83	5.16	5.86	5.84	4.99	6.56	6.82
3 yr.	0.08	7.68	5.49	5.32	4.71	7.89	5.28	6.03	5.87	5.05	6.66	6.83
4 yr.	0.07	7.92	5.64	5.90	5.05	7.88	5.40	6.17	5.91	5.10	6.71	6.84
5 yr.	0.06	8.06	6.29	6.14	5.29	7.86	5.50	6.27	5.95	5.15	6.75	6.85
6 yr.	0.06	8.19	6.50	6.33	5.46	7.88	5.57	6.33	5.97	5.19	6.79	6.86
7 yr.	0.05	8.31	6.71	6.52	5.63	7.89	5.64	6.39	5.98	5.21	6.82	6.88
8 yr.	0.05	8.33	6.83	6.61	5.73	7.89	5.69	6.44	6.00	5.25	6.87	6.89
9 yr.	0.04	8.35	6.95	6.71	5.84	7.89	5.74	6.48	6.02	5.29	6.90	6.89
10 yr.	0.42	8.37	7.07	6.81	5.95	7.89	5.79	6.53	6.03	5.31	6.93	6.90
10 yr. Amort. base rate (vintage specific)		8.26	6.76	6.54	5.71	7.88	5.69	6.43	6.00	5.26	6.87	6.89

Table A3 Liquidity premium schedules for various vintages (1996–2006)

Liquidity premium for various vintages

Term	Principal drop	1996	1997	1998	1999	2000	2001	2002	2003	2004	2005	2006
1 mo.		0.000	0.000	0.000	0.000	0.000	0.000	0.000	0.000	0.001	0.001	0.000
1 yr.	0.09	0.004	0.001	0.000	0.003	0.002	0.004	0.002	0.001	0.001	0.000	0.003
2 yr.	0.08	0.006	0.005	0.004	0.006	0.005	0.006	0.004	0.006	0.006	0.005	0.004
3 yr.	0.08	0.008	0.008	0.006	0.007	0.007	0.008	0.007	0.008	0.010	0.005	0.008
4 yr.	0.07	0.012	0.011	0.011	0.007	0.010	0.009	0.009	0.011	0.007	0.008	0.008
5 yr.	0.06	0.011	0.012	0.011	0.011	0.012	0.011	0.011	0.014	0.011	0.012	0.012
6 yr.	0.06	0.016	0.014	0.015	0.013	0.015	0.014	0.012	0.015	0.014	0.016	0.014
7 yr.	0.05	0.017	0.016	0.016	0.016	0.017	0.016	0.017	0.016	0.016	0.016	0.016
8 yr.	0.05	0.016	0.018	0.021	0.019	0.021	0.020	0.017	0.017	0.019	0.018	0.017
9 yr.	0.04	0.020	0.021	0.021	0.019	0.019	0.020	0.019	0.019	0.021	0.020	0.022
10 yr.	0.42	0.022	0.022	0.021	0.020	0.022	0.023	0.022	0.021	0.022	0.022	0.022
10 yr. Amort. l.p. (vintage specific)		0.0189	0.0187	0.0187	0.0178	0.0189	0.0198	0.0185	0.0183	0.0188	0.0190	0.0191

Table A4 Vintage specific core FTP rates

Vintage specific core FTP rates

Term	Principal drop	1996	1997	1998	1999	2000	2001	2002	2003	2004	2005	2006
1mo.		7.69	4.69	3.31	3.25	6.00	5.69	5.50	5.72	5.07	5.82	6.63
1 yr.	0.09	7.32	4.23	3.99	3.75	7.49	5.30	5.64	5.81	4.98	6.31	6.89
2 yr.	0.08	7.40	4.90	4.74	4.31	7.84	5.16	5.86	5.85	4.99	6.56	6.82
3 yr.	0.08	7.68	5.50	5.33	4.71	7.89	5.28	6.04	5.88	5.06	6.66	6.83
4 yr.	0.07	7.93	5.65	5.91	5.06	7.89	5.41	6.17	5.92	5.11	6.72	6.85
5 yr.	0.06	8.07	6.30	6.15	5.31	7.88	5.51	6.28	5.96	5.16	6.76	6.86
6 yr.	0.06	8.20	6.52	6.34	5.47	7.89	5.58	6.34	5.98	5.21	6.80	6.88
7 yr.	0.05	8.33	6.73	6.53	5.64	7.91	5.65	6.41	6.00	5.23	6.84	6.89
8 yr.	0.05	8.35	6.85	6.63	5.75	7.91	5.71	6.45	6.02	5.27	6.89	6.90
9 yr.	0.04	8.37	6.97	6.73	5.86	7.91	5.76	6.50	6.04	5.31	6.92	6.91
10 yr.	0.42	8.39	7.09	6.83	5.97	7.91	5.81	6.55	6.05	5.33	6.95	6.92
10 yr. Amort.												
Core rate (vintage specific)		8.281	6.782	6.563	5.728	7.899	5.711	6.451	6.020	5.275	6.886	6.906

Budgeting, Performance Monitoring and Incentive Compensation

INTRODUCTION

The preparation of a budget or a plan[1] is a time-consuming exercise that almost all financial institutions go through every year, generally in Autumn. Finance professionals in a bank typically spend more time on budget preparation and discussions and monitoring of performance relative to plan than on any other activity, by a wide margin. The process of creating a budget for every fiscal year and periodically monitoring performance against that budget has existed in large organisations in general and financial institutions in particular since at least the 1950s. In most financial institutions, the total manpower and effort devoted to the process of budgeting and planning, not including the on-going efforts of monitoring performance, exceed those devoted to strategic planning. This fact is testimony to the importance of budgeting in a financial institution but is also a rather poor commentary on the institution's priorities.

In recent years, the budget process has come under criticism. Jack Welch, retired CEO of General Electric, called the budget the "bane of corporate America." In financial institutions, not only is it time consuming with not enough commensurate benefit but also it is subject to interminable discussions from negotiations in the formulation stage to finding faults in the shortfall stage. The reason for this is partly the nature of the compensation plan tied to budgetary targets and partly the fact that a single scenario budget is usually prepared. Most finance professionals are not used to forecasting contingent on probabilistic scenarios. Instead, they resort to what can be called "re-forecasting" based once again on *one* revised scenario. The result is known as a forecast in contrast to a budget or a plan.

Notwithstanding all the disadvantages of budgeting/planning, it remains at the core of financial planning, performance monitoring and is very relevant to determination of incentive compensation in a financial institution.

BUDGET AND FORECAST

The budget is prepared for a fiscal year generally in the Autumn of the year preceding. It is a once-a-year event and therefore static in nature. In a typical bank, the budget is a set of financial numbers for a *single* scenario. Sometimes the single scenario is supplemented by a worst-case and a best-case scenario. But such scenarios are typically not the result of analysis of the drivers that can potentially change but the result of stresses on the numbers in the base scenario.

The external financial world changes frequently. Therefore, the static budget usually becomes somewhat irrelevant even before the fiscal year has set in. The revisions (to the budgetary numbers) at different points in the fiscal year are known as *forecasts* in contrast to the budget or the plan. The latter is for twelve months. But the forecast can be for a period of the remaining months of the year or for any longer period, usually up to eighteen months forward.

Just as the budget, the forecast also consists of single scenario numbers. This is in contrast with contingent numbers for different scenarios with probabilities assigned to each scenario. A contingent cash flow approach to forecasting requires a good understanding of the fundamental drivers of the economy or the local market sector, which are not traditional accounting variables. It also requires an understanding of probabilities and sometimes the basics of simulation. Most finance professionals in a financial institution are not trained in these aspects.

ZERO-BASED BUDGETING

Traditionally, the budgeting process in a financial institution starts with the numbers contained in last year's (sometimes revised) budget. A target growth rate is set from the top. The simplest budget is trending the last year's budget numbers by incorporating the growth. In case the realised numbers in the last year were very different from the budget numbers than the starting point typically is last year's realised numbers. Looking at last year's budget and simply asking for more or less is not a very interesting exercise for the business unit managers but in most financial institutions they seem to gravitate to this lowest common denominator because it requires little thinking. Finance professionals, trained in the supremacy of numbers, prefer an internally self-consistent (ie, one that can be rolled up or down the hierarchy without any apparent inconsistency) budget to achieving higher risk-adjusted returns or higher operational efficiencies. Trending up (or down) last year's budget is a sure way of ensuring self-consistency since it was so the last year (or the year before).

Zero-based budgeting advocates building each year's budget based on needs (starting at US$0). This is clearly in contrast to traditional budgeting. Under zero-based budgeting each item of major expenditure in the budget has to be justified. Instead of a target growth rate, the organisation's objectives are spelt out, to which each existing or new item of expenditure must contribute in a meaningful way. The cost of each activity must be confirmed to be worth the investment at the expense of doing something else with the same amount of money. Therefore, zero-based budgeting requires looking at a set of alternative and comparing the cost of undertaking each alternative.

Zero-based budgeting is not an easy exercise. It requires a lot of analysis and comparison among alternatives. By definition, at every step it challenges the status-quo. It often involves choice which is confrontational. There is a strong tendency in financial institutions to avoid confrontation, even if it may lead to a better allocation of resources. Traditional trend-based budgeting favors existing functions and businesses while zero-based budgeting favors new and more profitable functions and businesses.

MONITORING OF PERFORMANCE

In Chapters 1 and 5, we have introduced many traditional and risk-adjusted performance measures used in a financial institution. There is no point in devising elaborate performance measures if they are not monitored periodically and indeed frequently. The purpose of frequent monitoring is the hope that pro-active corrective steps can be taken in time. In a large financial institution with multi-product lines, it takes some effort to pull together so many performance measures up the hierarchy.

In almost all financial institutions, monitoring of performance is not done in absolute terms. For most important performance measures, monitoring is done by comparing actual performance on that particular measure to the planned target. The budget or the plan specifically states the expected value of the performance measure every month or quarter along the way for the full fiscal year. These are referred to as targets. It is generally true that not all performance measures have specific targets spelled out in the budget.

The rank and file finance professionals in a bank spend an inordinate amount of time and effort in monitoring actual performance against planned targets. The most common means by which the results are reported by them and discussed is known as variance analysis, which is described in the next section. It is not their responsibility to correct shortfalls in performance. Generally speaking, the finance function in a financial institution does not operate as a strategic partner of the business units.

Performance monitoring is, therefore, very much an *ex-post* exercise in the traditional mode of command and control. Modern enterprise-wide performance measurement systems with management reporting tools have made it easier and quicker for everyone to get the same information thus reducing the pain of both budgeting and performance monitoring. But the essential philosophy of central control is still at the core of the budget. This stifles entrepreneurial activity at various parts of the organisation.

PERFORMANCE RELATIVE TO PLAN AND VARIANCE ANALYSIS

As mentioned before, a single scenario budget is never going to be realised as such. The budgeting process takes months. In the meantime, the financial world changes so rapidly, that the budget needs change even before it has been finalised. Therefore for any item in the budget, the actual amount will vary from the planned amount. For some the actual may exceed plan and for some the actual may fall short of plan. The means by which this difference between actual and planned numbers is analysed is called variance analysis.

Variance analysis is not just a post-mortem. Its value lies in what variances are trying to tell management about the behaviour and performance of the various components of the business. There are very few plans that turn out exactly as predicted. Even when the overall objectives of the plan are achieved, some, if not all components of the performance will have varied from the sub-plans or standards that make up the overall picture. For example, an athletic team may win an important game, as planned, but within the team performance there may be many aspects that the coach will analyse during and after the match so that performance can be improved for next time. As in business, good points need to be encouraged, less positive aspects need to be discussed and corrected. There is little to be gained for the next year if we do not think about the last year's performance in detail. Variance analysis provides a framework for business managers to breakdown the overall performance of an organisation, so that each individual element of the business can be isolated and analysed in turn.

In order to do variance analysis effectively, one has to know what level of variance is meaningful, or material, to the business. This is called developing a *materiality* threshold. Missing a revenue target by US$50,000 might not mean much to a business unit that makes billions of dollars in annual revenue, but it would be a lot more material to a smaller business unit.

After the concept of materiality comes the concept of *context*. Context is the relationship of the variance to the type of measurement. For example, if a business unit generates 10% more demand deposit volume in April than it did in March, a simple explanation in a month-to-month context is that the business is growing. But, considering factors such as seasonality, it would be more appropriate to measure against the previous year's April volume to see how the business unit did in the context of tax seasons. If demand deposit volume dropped from the previous April, the variance analysis would let one know to look for a more specific cause than month-to-month growth.

Recognising the materiality threshold for the business and adjusting the context of the analysis helps one recognise important variance levels and find the real causes and trends of variance. This knowledge can then be applied to improve the institution's financial plans.

A financial budget is not expressed in terms of one financial measure but progressively in terms of several financial measures.

These measures, almost by definition, do not necessarily go in the same direction. Therefore, when the realised results are observed, they may exceed the budget in terms of some of the financial measures and be short of the budgeted numbers in terms of the other financial measures. Variance analysis item by item can easily be done but a picture of overall variance is difficult to obtain. A DuPont analysis of performance ratios like return on equity (see Appendix in Chapter 1) helps in understanding the variance analysis. Breaking up a performance measure into its drivers (eg, Figure 1 of Chapter 5) also helps in understanding the variance analysis.

With the advent of activity-based costing (introduced in Chapter 4), variance analysis of actual *versus* budget have become more root-cause analysis. This is called *Diagnostic Variance Analysis*. Budget variances are analysed in terms of the activity-based components that make up the variance, and evaluated in light of overall business performance. As a result of this type of analysis, the underlying cause of the variance is revealed, providing the necessary business insight to make sound strategic decisions (see Ramsey 1999 for more details).

INCENTIVE COMPENSATION

Employees in financial institutions receive four types of compensation: (i) salary, (ii) benefits, (iii) incentive compensation (or bonus) and (iv) stock options/restricted stocks. The compensations of executives are weighted heavily by the last item, which is viewed as long-term incentive. But for the vast majority of employees in a financial institution the first three are the ones that matter. While salary and benefits are predetermined, incentive compensation (IC) is dependent on performance. In many cases the relationship between IC and performance measure(s) is formulaic and pre-determined while in others IC is ad-hoc and decided *ex-post*. Theoretically, IC should reward specific results beyond routine job performance.

It is sometimes said that in a large and multi-business financial institution, a compensation system may be a more powerful driver of its performance than the chief executive or the culture of the organisation. A poorly designed IC plan can result in vast amounts of wasted activity and foregone value creation. Yet few financial institutions properly align their IC plans to long-term objectives of the organisation.

The four performance related concepts: appropriate performance measures, budgeting, performance monitoring and IC should not be confused with one another. Nor is any one a substitute for another. It can, however, be argued that a well-designed set of performance metrics which effectively convey corporate strategy throughout most of the organization (see Chapter 10 on balanced scorecards) can lead to superior performance and then higher IC will automatically follow. This notion is yet to be tested at large financial institutions especially in institutions which have traditionally followed a formulaic IC plan. Suffice it to say, however, that it is much better than a poorly designed IC formula. Expanding on Kane (2002), we can provide a laundry list of guiding principles for designing a good incentive compensation program in a financial institution:

❑ Start by identifying the institution's strategic profit drivers.
❑ Keep it simple.
❑ Recognise up-front that IC plan is not a substitute for good management.
❑ Tie individual compensation to business unit performance.
❑ Avoid items on which the individual or business unit has no control.
❑ As far as possible, base IC on improvement of the performance measure(s) rather than on budgeted value of the measure(s).
❑ Set thresholds which are neither too ambitious nor too low.
❑ Provide regular, accurate reporting of results.
❑ Test, evaluate, refine.

A typical IC plan in a financial institution consists first of determination of a high level "IC pool" and attribution of the pool through several lower level IC plans. A typical (somewhat simplified since IC usually depends on more than one performance measure) IC plan looks like the following Figure 1.

There is one major drawback to this kind of IC plan. The cost of under-performance is perceived as significantly greater than the benefit of over-performance. Consequently, if it becomes clear to the business unit managers that they will fall well below target, they will begin to defer revenues as much as possible and accelerate expenses as much as possible. This is done in order to protect next year's IC since current year's IC will be zero in any case. In the other extreme, if targets are in danger of being overachieved

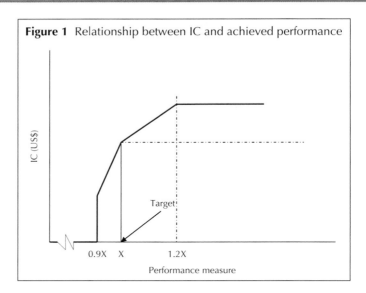

Figure 1 Relationship between IC and achieved performance

considerably, revenues will again be deferred and expenses accelerated. This is done in order to assure a higher IC next year while the maximum IC this year is already assured.

The pivotal role paid by the target value of the performance measure in the IC plan leads to "negotiations" during the budget process (not negotiation of the IC plan as such) in which managers deliberately reduce targets below what they can conceivably achieve. Executive management's desire to "stretch" targets is anticipated by managers during the budget negotiation process. This process ends up rewarding the best negotiator rather than the best performer.

---

1   The terms "budget" and "plan" are often used synonymously, although subtle distinctions are made by some finance professionals. Plan is a broader term with budget defined as the expression of a plan in financial terms. We, however, will use them to mean the same thing. Both are static and prepared for the fiscal year.

REFERENCES

Kane, M., 2002, "Creating Incentive Programs that Drive the Right Results", mimeo, Kane Bank Services, October. www.kanebankservices.com

Ramsey, T. L., 1999, "Diagnostic Variance Analysis", *The Journal of Bank Cost & Management Accounting*.

10

From Financial Performance Measures to Balanced Scorecards

INTRODUCTION

In Chapter 1 we have discussed the numerous traditional performance measures in use in a financial institution. All these measures are by and large financial measures. With the steady erosion of franchises and geographically restricted banking, a financial institution has to basically take risk in order to generate returns. Risk in financial instruments, particularly with contingent cash flows, is very complex to understand and to measure. It is natural that only recently have risk-adjusted performance measures (RAPM) taken root in the financial industry. In fact, many financial institutions are only going through the process of introducing such RAPM(s) and getting them ingrained into the culture of the organisation. Ironically, the impetus has come less from the understanding that risk and return are inherently intertwined and that the effects of risk in particular manifest themselves over long periods and more from the pressure to create shareholder value.

While the financial industry is in the process of dealing with RAPMs, the traditional financial measures have been barraged with another school of thought, which in its extreme might argue: "Make operational improvements and the numbers will follow." However, the original proponents of this school of thought (see Kaplan and Norton, 1992, from which the above quote is taken) do not advocate replacement of financial performance measures by operational performance measures. Reliance on one set of measures to the exclusion of others is neither balanced nor optimal.

Hence the term *Balanced Scorecard*. Balanced Scorecard (BSC) has been first introduced in industrial organisations and has only recently taken root in large financial institutions in the US.

Ironically middle level managers in financial institutions in the US have long taken one or more measures of operational efficiency into account in day to day management. However, in most high level performance review discussions, financial performance relative to budget has been the focus. It is the lack of understanding of executive management in US financial institutions about continuous improvement and the fundamental principles underlying balanced scorecard that BSC is treated as a panacea. Perhaps as with society at large, executive management keeps looking for dramatic events, which mergers and acquisition are but continuous improvement is not. Yet the latter is of far more consequence to value creation than the former.

WHAT IS A BALANCED SCORECARD?

In their original article,[1] Kaplan and Norton (1992) outlined a simple *four-box approach* to performance measurement. To take a *"balanced"* view of the company's performance, in addition to financial measures, executives need to take into account measures drawn from three other *"perspectives"* of the business. The four perspectives are:

Financial perspective – measures reflecting financial performance. These measures can be traditional measures like return on assets, earnings per share or RAPM like economic value added.

Customer perspective – measures having a direct impact on customers, for example time taken to process a phone call, results of customer surveys, number of complaints or competitive rankings.

Internal Business process perspective – measures reflecting the performance of key business processes, for example the time spent prospecting, number of units that required rework or process cost. These are not financial costs but are more efficiency measures.

Innovation and Learning perspective – measures describing the company's learning curve for example, number of employee suggestions or total hours spent on staff training.

Along each of these perspectives, performance goals and performance measures can be defined and monitored from time to time. The best way to explain how this is done is to provide illustrations

Table 1 ABC bank's balanced scorecard

Financial perspective		Internal business process perspective	
Goals	**Measures**	**Goals**	**Measures**
Growth	Year over year revenue growth	Leverage technology	Common platform for customer information
	Year over year *earnings per share* growth		Capacity utilisation
Shareholder value creation	Economic value added	Continuous improvement	Six sigma metrics
Customer perspective		**Innovation and learning perspective**	
Goals	**Measures**	**Goals**	**Measures**
Customer satisfaction	Customer survey scores	Quality workforce	Employee development
	Market share		Turnover
			Employee survey scores
Customer retention	Existing customer attrition rate	Empowerment	# of successful employee suggestions

of hypothetical BSCs for financial institutions. Table 1 below is an illustrative bank's BSC.

Along the financial perspective, the measures are generally well-defined and numerically measured. With the advent of six-sigma and ABC (see Chapter 4 for details including references) which preceded BSC, measures along the internal business process perspective can also be quantitatively defined and measured. Along the other two perspectives, however, the measures may not be so quantitative.

A financial institution's BSC can be more specific than the illustration in Table 1 above contains. Target and acceptable ranges of the measures can be spelt out in the BSC. Also initiatives that are supposed to help the organisation reach the goal can be included. The following Tables 2 and 3 below contain another illustrative bank's BSC.

An emphasis on initiatives and making one person responsible for coordinating and monitoring progress on the initiatives are convenient and common, though hackneyed, management practices in large organisations. It only goes to prove the fundamental

Table 2 XYZ commercial bank's balanced scorecard

Goal	Measure	Target(s)	Acceptable	Initiative
Financial perspective				
Growth	Year over year revenue growth	10%	8%	Targeted marketing campaign
Shareholder value creation	Economic value added	US$500 mm in Yr 1 US$600 mm in Yr 2	US$350 mm in Yr 1 US$500 mm in Yr 2	Known as an EVA company
Revenue mix	Fee Income/ spread income	30% in Yr 1 40% in Yr 2	25% in Yr 1 32.5% in Yr 2	Integration of investment banking and commercial banking
Customer perspective				
Deep customer Relationship	Share of customers with three or more products	35% in Yr 1 40% in Yr 2	30% in Yr 1 35% in Yr 2	Cross-sell initiative
Customer Retention	Existing customer attrition rate	<25% in Yr 1 <20% in Yr 2	<30% in Yr 1 <25% in Yr 2	Proactive customer complaint monitoring

Table 3 XYZ commercial bank's balanced scorecard (continued)

Goal	Measure	Targets	Acceptable	Initiative
Internal business process perspective				
Leverage technology	Common platform for customer information	9 out of 12 systems in Yr 1 12 systems in Yr 2	7 out of 12 systems in Yr 1 12 systems in Yr 2	Data warehouse project
Information based strategy	Use of analytics	60% of all solicitations based on analytics in Yr 1 All solicitations based on analytics in Yr 2	Data mining and solicitation experiments 80% solicitations based on analytics in Yr 2	Strategic analytics
Innovation and learning perspective				
Quality workforce	Employee turnover	<25% in Yr 1 <20% in Yr 2	30% in Yr 1 35% in Yr 2	Employee first year experience project

weakness of the organisation that every significant performance improvement has to come through an "initiative."

CASCADING DOWN A BALANCED SCORECARD PROCESS
Building a corporate-level balanced scorecard is a semi-academic exercise, most of which can be done by a consultant interviewing the top executives of a corporation. If the latter were to sit back and read some conceptual literature on management, the corporate balanced scorecard customised to the organisation in question can easily be prepared internally. A much more difficult and critical element in the implementation of a balanced scorecard is the way it is *cascaded* down the organisational hierarchy.

If we limit ourselves to the financial perspective, traditional accounting numbers are additive. It is, therefore, easy to roll up or down such financial measures and monitored almost the same way at most levels of the institution. This statement is not as true in the case of non-traditional financial measures (RAPMs) but still with the introduction of some additional complexity, a sensible cascading can be achieved. Along the other three perspectives, however, the task is far from easy in a financial institution.

In operational terms and in customer interfaces, the different units in a financial institution vary considerably, much more so than in a manufacturing organisation. Therefore, the measures that are critical along the customer perspective, internal business process perspective and innovation and learning perspective can be quite different from one business unit to another. Even if all of them have ordinal scores (in contrast to cardinal values), they are not additive. One simple but impractical way of dealing with it is to roll up each of these to the next higher level. It is impractical because soon the BSCs at high level hierarchy points and the corporate BSC become extremely unwieldy. However, conceptual and qualitative connections can be usually derived between each of these seemingly diverse measures at the lower level BSC and one (or two) single measure at the next higher level BSC. This is where a lot of thought and extreme care are needed to think through such connections, which do not come from analysis and rarely come from outside the organisation. The knowledge of banking in general and the various causes and effects within the institution in particular are the mainstay of this most difficult part of building a good BSC framework throughout the different levels of a financial institution.

To illustrate how BSC is woven together between one level and the next, the following Tables 4 and 5 illustrate how the corporate BSC of Tables 2 and 3 is cascaded a level below. We have chosen to focus on the Risk Unit(s) within the financial institution (a commercial bank).

A balanced scorecard need not be "balanced" in the sense that all the performance measures along all four perspectives are given equal importance. Prior to mid-1990's performance measures in all organisations was so predominantly financial that a "balance" was needed by placing non-financial measures at par with financial measures. In most financial institutions performance measurement is still heavily tilted towards financial measures so that it is necessary to bring about a balance by introducing and focusing on the other non-financial perspectives. Once a BSC program is put in place, financial measures may still remain the most important ones but they are no longer the only ones. The insistence on similar if not

Table 4 XYZ commercial bank: risk units' balanced scorecard

Corporate goal	Business unit objective	Measure	Target	Acceptable
Financial perspective				
Economic value added	Minimise losses	Net charge-off (NCO)	30 bps Yr 1 20 bps in Yr 2	50 bps in Yr 1 25 bps in Yr 2
	Cure problem loans in time	Non-performing (NPL) ratio	50 bps in Yr 1 35 bps in Yr 2	80 bps in Yr 1 40 bps in Yr 2
Customer perspective				
Customer satisfaction	Minimise regulatory issues	Disposal of pending issues	90% of issues within the specified date	80% of issues within a month of the specified date
		CAMEL rating	Rating of 1 for asset quality, liquidity and sensitivity to market risk	Rating of 1 or 2 for asset quality, liquidity and sensitivity to market risk
	Internal customer (other units of the bank) satisfaction	Customer satisfaction survey Score	Average score of 4 or more (in a scale of 1 to 5)	Average score of 3 or more (in a scale of 1 to 5)

Table 5 XYZ bank: risk units' balanced scorecard (continued)

Corporate goal	Business unit objective	Measure	Target	Acceptable
Internal business process perspective				
Information based strategy	Common data mart for Risk variables	Proportion of risk variables available at one place for analysis	Feed from 9 out of 12 systems to risk data mart in Yr 1 Feed from all 12 systems to risk data mart in Yr 2	Feed from 7 out of 12 systems to risk data mart in Yr 1 Feed from all 12 systems to risk data mart in Yr 2
	Sophisticated underwriting based on analytics	# of distinct scorecards in use	5 to 6 additional scorecards in Yr 1 Underwriting of all major credit products using analytics by Yr 3	9 to 10 additional scorecards in Yrs 1 and 2 Underwriting of all major credit products using analytics by Yr 3
Innovation and learning perspective				
Quality workforce	Workforce institutional memory	Employee Turnover # of employees with experience of last recession	<25% in Yr 1 <20% in Yr 2 50%	30% in Yr 1 35% in Yr 2 40%

equal importance being placed on all the measures in the BSC is a misconception of the term "balanced" in balanced scorecard.

Another misconception is of the term "scorecard" in balanced scorecard. It does not imply that all the measures in a BSC are *quantitative*. In principle, performance measures in a BSC can be *qualitative*. Performance monitoring in financial institutions are notoriously focused on comparing performance to targets and to those of peer institutions. This mantra is not likely to change even after the introduction of BSC. Such comparisons are, no doubt, harder to make with qualitative measures than with quantitative measures.

BALANCED SCORECARD FOR STRATEGIC MANAGEMENT

In addition to balancing performance measures monitored at different levels, a balanced scorecard has been posited as a cornerstone of a strategic management system (see Kaplan and Norton,

1998). A BSC is a means of enabling a company to focus the entire organisation on implementing long-term strategy. But is it really?

A financial institution's operational and management performance monitoring is built around short-term budgetary targets and has little to do with achieving its long-term strategic priorities. In another chapter we have introduced the shareholder value creation paradigm. This paradigm needs new financial performance measures to supplement if not replace traditional financial measures which, at least in the way they have been monitored, are by and large, short-term. Even if a financial institution has non-financial performance measures that are monitored, such monitoring system is typically short-term and just as inadequate for achieving long-term strategic goals. A BSC shifts the emphasis of performance measurement from only financial measures to wider perspectives. But BSC has very little to do with changing the short-term focus to strategic focus.

The BSC can rightly be viewed as a *management system* and not a measurement system only, that enables organisations to clarify their vision and strategy and translate them into action. However, every performance measurement and monitoring system is consistent with a broader management system. What is measured and monitored is what an organisation gets – this is true at the business unit level as well as the corporate level. A BSC framework can be built following the four perspectives and cascaded down (where the most intelligence is needed) with care, throughout a financial institution. It will only reflect the culture of the organisation. If it is the short-term that drives the culture of the rank and file of the institution, even a very good and faithful implementation of a company-wide BSC will not achieve long-term strategic objectives. If executives in an institution lack the ability to take strategic views and anticipate major market changes, a good BSC cannot be a substitute.

In a financial institution, mergers with and acquisitions of other institutions or portfolios are sometimes considered the lion's share of strategy formulation and execution. The success of a merger or an acquisition has a big impact on an institution's performance as well as on personnel but the average merger or acquisition probably erodes rather than creates shareholder value. A BSC is not particularly helpful in thinking through synergies of potential mergers or in effecting a smooth integration post merger. Strategic thinking and execution are much more enduring and much less common skills than bringing about a merger or an acquisition. Given that distinctive strategic thinking exists and is encouraged in the institution, BSC can be a valuable tool for execution. It provides a ready-made mechanism of cascading performance measurement and monitoring down each level that are consistent with the high level strategy. Since what is measured and monitored is what an organisation gets, the BSC provides a way of ensuring that all parts of the organisation are working towards something relevant to them but is also positively contributing to achievement of the strategy. But absent true strategic thinking, product innovation and market anticipation, BSC will remain just another unsuccessful tool in a financial institution.

We have mentioned before that (numerical) financial measures are, by and large, not greatly difficult to cascade up and down through all levels of the institution in an analytically consistent manner. The statement is also true when we are dealing with performance measured in quantities and distances, which is rare in a financial institution. An example in a somewhat different setting is what has come to be known as Kantorovich[2] method in resource allocation in command planning in erstwhile USSR. The long-term performance of USSR planned economy was dismal not because there was anything wrong with the inter-relationships cascading through the levels of the Soviet planned economy that Kantorovich devised but because of poor strategies on the part of the powers that be. The same is true of a large organisation and particularly so with a multi-product and multi-channel financial institution. The concept of a tool like BSC and the intelligence that goes into conceptually connecting measures and their drivers at different levels while cascading a BSC framework are valid ones and not to be confused with, or blamed for, the lack of clear strategic thinking on the part of executives leading the complex organisation.

Contrary to intuition, the cascading of a BSC need not endeavour to explain organisational strategies to all levels by translating them in terminology they understand. In fact below a certain level, the corporate strategy or strategies need not even be propagated. It is far more important to figure out one or two measures that (i) units at that level can relate to in terms of what they do on a day-to-day basis, and (ii) are consistent with and help improve the measures of success of the corporate strategy or strategies. Once that is done, it is prudent to let them achieve the best they can with those one or two measures and not worry about whether they understand or speak in terms of corporate strategies. As stated before, *cascading* is the most important element of BSC in general and for the use of BSC in executing strategies in particular. Just as total quality management (TQM), this is best done by thought leaders amongst insiders who are immersed in the day-to-day running of the organisation than by outsiders.

CONCLUSION

Over almost the whole of the twentieth century, corporate performance has focused primarily on financial measures. This has been particularly so for financial institutions. Even the most common day-to-day functions in a financial institution involve numbers and it may be understandable why financial measures are so very overwhelming in a financial institution. In the last couple of decades of the twentieth century financial institutions in the US have been facing more and more competition – with the liberalisation of many of the restrictions, geographic or otherwise, on expansion of financial services. At the same time have come more and more automation and dependence on customer information. Consequently, efficient operation, high customer satisfaction, innovative new product development are some of the important ways for a financial institution to distinguish itself. Focusing only or predominantly on financial metrics for performance measurement and monitoring is no longer enough.

Balanced Scorecard (BSC) is a concept of performance measurement that balances financial measures with non-financial ones. A "balanced" view of an institution looks upon performance from four perspectives:

❑ Financial perspective
❑ Customer perspective
❑ Internal Business process perspective and
❑ Innovation and Learning perspective.

While these have become the usual four dimensions and have been used in this chapter and its examples, a larger set of non-financial perspectives may be used. The central idea is to bring about a balance between financial and non-financial performance measures. However, it does not mean that all measures along all dimensions have to be equally important. In a financial institution, some financial measures continue to be more important than many operational measures but not at the exclusion of the latter. Also performance measures in a BSC can be qualitative as well quantitative.

BSC is not just for corporate level performance but also for internal business unit performance. Most of the benefits of having a balanced scorecard cannot be derived unless it is implemented at various levels of the organisation. The most critical element in the implementation of a balanced scorecard in a financial institution is the way it is *cascaded* down the organisational hierarchy. A lot of thought goes into deriving conceptual and qualitative connections between each of many seemingly diverse measures at the lower level BSC and one (or two) single measure at the next higher level BSC.

The BSC is more generally a management system that enables organisations to clarify their vision and strategy and translate them into action. Notwithstanding the emphasis on financial performance measures in US financial institutions, middle level managers have long taken one or more measure of operational efficiency into account in day to day management. BSC is a conceptual means of formalising that. Given that distinctive strategic thinking exists and is encouraged in the institution, BSC provides a way of ensuring that all parts of the organisation are working towards something relevant to them and also positively contributing to achievement of the strategy. On the other hand, if executives in an institution lack the ability to take strategic views and anticipate major market changes, a good BSC can never be a substitute.

1   The first balanced scorecard was developed at Analog Devices Inc. in 1987–88 but it was popularised as a concept by Kaplan and Norton. See Schneiderman (2001) for details of the first balanced scorecard.
2   For a non-technical description of Kantorovich method, which was later further advanced into what is known as *linear programming*, see Kantorovich's Nobel lecture (1975) and for more technical details see Kantorovich (1960).

REFERENCES

Kantorovich, L. V., 1960, "The Mathematical Method of Production Planning and Organization", *Management Science*, **6(4)**, July, pp 363–422.

Kantorovich, L. V., 1975, "Nobel Lecture", at the website http://nobelprize.org/nobel_prizes/economics/laureates/1975/kantorovich-autobio.html

Kaplan, R. S. and D. P. Norton, 1992, "The Balanced Scorecard – Measures that Drive Performance", *Harvard Business Review*, January–Feburary, pp 71–80.

Kaplan, R. S. and D. P. Norton, 1998, "Using the Balanced Scorecard as a Strategic Management System", chapter in *Harvard Business Review on Measuring Corporate Performance*, Boston, Harvard Business School Press, pp 183–211.

Schneiderman, A. M., 2001, "The First Balanced Scorecard", *Journal of Cost Management*, **15(5)**, September–October, p 16.

11

Basel II and Improved Financial and Operational Performance

INTRODUCTION

The Basel II Accord, more formally, *"International Convergence of Capital Measurement and Capital Standards – A Revised Framework"* (Basel 2004) is the second international accord that has revised the international standards for the adequacy of a bank's capital. The first, much simpler, one was in 1988 (Basel I). Unlike Basel I, the new accord goes well beyond capital adequacy into measurement and management of risk and disclosure.

As can be expected the Basel II Accord has numerous provisions and covers the whole gamut of risk characteristics and allows for both simplified and advanced approaches. The Accord is separated into three Pillars. They add up to a very large document. This chapter can only provide a bird's eye view of the contents of the Basel II Accord. However, it focuses on those elements of Basel II that point beyond regulatory compliance and even risk management to improved performance, both financial and operational.

Basel II aligns regulatory capital closer to economic capital. In doing so, its requirements force a bank to focus on relevant data and analytics as main drivers of risk measurement and management. Economic capital is at the core of new financial performance measures that are better aligned to shareholder value creation. Basel II almost created a whole new field of operational risk. The elements of the Basel II advanced approach in operational risk are now the best practice in operational risk management, some of which can be used for process improvement and operational process efficiency. The data requirements of Basel II coupled with customer relationship management tools can pave the way for analytics based strategies. Such strategies, well executed, can give a bank a distinct competitive advantage.

WHAT IS BASEL II?

The Basel Committee on Banking Supervision (BCBS), was created to promote greater consistency in the way banks and banking regulators approach risk management across national borders. BCBS came up with its first bank capital adequacy standards (Basel I) in 1988 which was primarily meant for a "level playing field" amongst banks in the G10 countries. It has, however, been adopted over time by countries well beyond the G10.

Eleven years down the line, it was felt strongly that the Basel I provisions were too simplistic, were not sensitive enough to risk and completely inadequate for the progressively complex products and portfolios held by internationally active banks. Furthermore, banks in general disclose very little information about the risk composition of their portfolios or their operational risks and controls for stock investors to take a very informed view of a particular bank.

The Basel Committee issued the first consultative paper in 1999 followed by a much more comprehensive consultative paper in January 2001 and finally the third consultative paper in April 2003, which has come to be known as CP3 (Basel 2003b). Further changes made in some provisions in 2004 resulting in what is called the Accord or the Revised Framework (Basel 2004). This framework and some additions made in 2005 have been incorporated in the document *International Convergence of Capital Measurement and Capital Standards* (Basel 2006) – which also includes the elements of the 1988 Accord that were not revised during Basel II. This document can, therefore, be treated as the comprehensive Basel II Accord or the "New Accord".

In these years of formulation, the Basel II Accord proposals have changed significantly and evolved as a complex set of recommendations that span from capital adequacy formulae to regulatory approval of methodology to responsibility of the bank's senior management and the Board to disclosure requirements. The implementation deadline is 2008 in general. However, enforcement of the new rules is the prerogative of the local regulator. On the one hand, some countries like India or China with not so well-developed bank risk management practice will follow a longer time-frame of implementation. In the US, on the other hand, Basel II is "mandatory" only for the largest ten banks or so.[1]

Basel II provides a range of options for determining the capital requirements for credit risk and operational risk to allow banks and supervisors to select approaches that are most appropriate for their operations and their financial market infrastructure. In the advanced approach of the new Accord is a significant innovation – the reliance on assessments of risk provided by banks' internal systems as inputs to capital calculations. Simultaneously, Basel II also put forward a detailed set of minimum requirements designed to ensure the integrity of these internal risk assessments.

The Basel II Accord consists of *three* inter-connected Pillars. The *First Pillar* sets out minimum regulatory capital requirements – the amount of capital banks must hold against risks. The methodology and formulae of the First Pillar of Basel II bring regulatory capital calculations much closer to economic capital calculations. In the process Basel II has given a boost to banks' focus on managing economic capital. Chapter 3 dwells on the basic concepts of economic capital and how it forms the main building block for new performance measurements that are better aligned to shareholder value creation. Thus, over time, Basel II presents banks with an opportunity to gain competitive advantage by allocating capital to those processes, segments, and markets that demonstrate a strong risk/return ratio. Developing a better understanding of the risk/reward trade-off for capital supporting specific businesses, customers, products and processes is one of the most important potential business benefits banks may derive from Basel II.

The *Second Pillar* of Basel II deals with the Supervisory Review Process. Supervisors are expected to evaluate how well banks are assessing their capital needs relative to their risks and to intervene, where appropriate. The supervisory review process is intended not only to ensure that banks have adequate capital to support all the risks in their business, but also to encourage banks to develop and use better risk management techniques in monitoring and managing their risks.

The *Third Pillar* of Basel II aims to bolster market discipline through enhanced disclosure by banks. At present precious little is known by the investor community about the risk and other characteristics of a bank's portfolio that says anything about the future risk of the bank. Basel II seeks to provide the much needed transparency in a manner that is comparable across institutions. At the same time, the Basel Committee has sought to ensure that the Basel II disclosure framework aligns with national accounting standards – and, in fact, does not conflict with broader accounting disclosure standards with which banks must comply.

Non-bank financial institutions are outside the scope of the Basel II Accord and will not face its compliance challenges immediately. But they are nonetheless likely to be pushed to use it as a competitive benchmark. These include insurance companies, financial arms of industrial companies, automobile captives and even asset management firms.

Calculating capital requirements under Basel II Accord requires a bank to implement a comprehensive risk management framework across the institution. The advanced approaches in Basel II requiring sophisticated data-based risk management may be rewarded[2] by lower capital requirements. However, these large implementation projects also will have wide-ranging effects on a bank's information technology systems and processes and on customer information. It is prudent for financial institutions to look upon Basel II from a perspective beyond regulatory compliance and even risk management to improved performance, both financial and operational. A KPMG Basel II-related document (KPMG 2004), which calls Basel II Accord a "A revolution disguised as regulation", conveys this point succinctly:

> More important, however, than the regulatory issues are the wide range of business implications and risk management challenges that the New (Basel II) Accord will trigger for banks, their non-bank competitors, customers, rating agencies, regulators, and, ultimately, the global capital markets. For example:
> ❑ Banks will be asked to implement an enterprise-wide risk management framework that ties regulatory capital to economic capital.
> ❑ Non-banks outside the scope of Basel II will not face its compliance challenges but may nonetheless be pushed to use it as a competitive benchmark.

❑ Banks will need to collect and disclose new information and face the implications of increased transparency.
❑ Rating agencies have new prominence as a result of the Basel II framework and thus could experience new competition.
❑ Regulators are challenged to provide a level playing field in their jurisdictions and internationally as the Basel Committee's recommendations are implemented by legislatures in various countries. In addition, regulators need to ensure that their examiners are adequately trained to assess bank's compliance with the new capital rules.
❑ The global banks could experience extended trends toward increased securitization as financial institutions adapt to Basel II requirements.

BASEL II, CREDIT RISK AND IMPROVED FINANCIAL PERFORMANCE

Basel II has two approaches to calculating capital for portfolio credit risk in senior lending: Standardised and Internal Ratings Based (IRB). It is the latter that is complex, analytical, data-based and calls for significant improvements in almost all financial institutions' risk management and information technology systems. At the same time, it is the IRB approach that holds promise for significant improvement in risk-adjusted performance. In most of what follows in this section, we have drawn upon Kofman (2004).

The provisions and requirements of the Basel II IRB approach essentially consist of good risk management practice both at the loan level and at the portfolio level or business unit level. To quote Kofman (2004):

At the loan level

❑ *Differentiating between risky borrowers (PD)* The IRB approach mandates that banks separate borrowers by riskiness in a way that is quantified and meaningful. Today, many banks unintentionally assign the same ratings to borrowers with different levels of risk. At the same time, internal ratings systems driven by inconsistent credit processes are often unable to identify variations in riskiness between seemingly like borrowers. In this way, the less risky borrowers in the rating grade are subsidising the greater risk of the others, because their capital requirements and loan pricing also fail to reflect risk differences. The bank is likely not getting paid for taking on this extra risk and may also be driving good business away if other institutions can differentiate risk better. In the IRB regulations this assessment of borrower risk is referred to as a probability of default (PD).

❏ *Differentiating the risk of the facility (LGD)* Similarly, most banks do not adequately distinguish between differences in the quality of loan facilities. IRB requires not only that the facility be rated separately from the risk of the borrower, but also that the bank has distinct and differentiated facility rating grades. The regulations refer to this rating as a loss given default (LGD). IRB recognises that the underwriting bank has the power to structure loan facilities to improve its repayment likelihood via covenants, collateral and security. While a revamped facility rating system will initially expose significant gaps in facility pricing and risky concentration of collateral, in the medium term this insight should lead to better management of facility risk.

❏ *Improved provisioning* By combining the borrower (PD) and facility (LGD) risk ratings, the bank can refine the way it provisions for expected losses. Accurate borrower-specific and facility-specific risk information, even if it results in the same portfolio-level of provision, will give management a clearer view of the more and less attractive facilities and sub-portfolios within the bank. The most important improvement from refined provisioning is the immediate impact on loan pricing. Over the longer term, as loans in the portfolio are re-rated and re-provisioned, the general provision will serve a rough guide to the risk level assumed by the bank and in business units within the institution. Combined with the bank's limit management system, this provides managers with leading indicators of portfolio-wide risk taking and clear candidates for improving that profile.

❏ *Improved pricing* Finally, and most importantly, loan-level risk differentiation can support differentiated pricing beyond the impact of an improved provision. This ability creates immediate bottom-line improvements, as many commercial loans are subject to annual renewal. Risk-based pricing provides a framework to identify earlier those revenue sources that appear attractive until subsequent risk outcomes wipe out the nominal revenues.

A risk-basis also allows the bank to demonstrate to customers and to management, that the price being offered on a loan is reasonable given the risk involved. If the customer pushes back on the offered price or maintains the competition is offering more favourable terms, management is in a position to justify its response. Accuracy in measuring the risk in lending, expressed in loan pricing, is becoming the critical element in bank competitive success.

At the portfolio level

❑ *The power of diversification* The risk-based relationship of a loan to its portfolio is grounded in correlation. A loan with low correlation to its fellow portfolio members can reduce its standalone risk-based economic capital requirement by up to 80% *versus* one with high correlation: The ability to estimate correlations on a differentiated basis allows a bank to refine its capital requirements. While this may not alter the overall capital requirement for the bank as a whole, it does allow a bank critical insight on which loans have the greatest impact on the portfolio in terms of reducing potential aggregate loss. This is important information to banks seeking to actively improve the portfolio's capital utilisation or return on capital through hedging or selling the riskiest or most capital-intensive loans.

❑ *Understanding the impact of concentrations* Many commercial defaults occur in bunches, driven by factors that affect a particular type of business and/or collateral type. For banks with a large portion of exposure to similar borrowers and collateral – what is referred to as having low diversification or high concentration – a flurry of defaults can have disastrous consequences on capital stability. For a bank with a diversified set of borrowers and collateral, these storms are smaller and easier to weather. In the ideal risk management world, diversification would mean the bank experiences very consistent and predictable credit losses every year. It is possible to measure the level of a portfolio's diversification. As noted in the preceding paragraph, it is possible to measure the impact each loan has on the portfolio's diversification and to include this impact in the pricing of the loan. The level of portfolio diversification – commonly referred to as correlation – can be as important to estimating risk-based pricing as the core metrics of PO and LGD for middle market loans.

❏ *Extending limits and capital* A well-diversified portfolio lowers the risk-based capital requirements on most of its loans. This has the effect of "freeing" up capital that was previously associated with the loans. This capital can then be re-deployed to new underwriting, essentially allowing the bank to increase its lending – and revenue – base without an accompanying capital increase. Likewise, it would allow a bank to be more competitive in pricing of loans where it could diversify away more of the risk (and the need for capital) or, if the bank did not have to compete on price, it could enjoy a better return on capital.

Chapter 3 of the book introduced economic capital as the cornerstone of enterprise risk management and economic capital based performance measures that seek to enhance shareholder value. The arguments above show how the measures required of Basel II IRB approach tie in with potentially better risk-adjusted performance of the credit portfolios. It is some of the same provisions of Basel II IRB that enables a bank to improve risk-adjusted performance through active portfolio management, as enumerated in Chapter 7.

BASEL II, OPERATIONAL RISK AND IMPROVED OPERATIONAL EFFICIENCY

Basel II has been the catalyst for significant developments in the whole new area of *operational risk*. As recently as 1999, *Derivatives Strategy* ran an article (Webb 1999) that there was no consensus in the industry on a precise definition of operational risk and concluded that such a consensus was unlikely to emerge in the near future. This would probably have been the case but for Basel II placing due emphasis on operational risk. It was not uncommon, at that point, to consider operational risk as a residual; everything other than credit risk or market risk was, by default, operational risk. Today, in keeping with semantics, we can call the residual concept as "other risk" in contrast with the concrete definition of operational risk that has emerged. An industry consensus defines operational risk as "the risk of direct or indirect loss resulting from inadequate or failed processes or systems, human factors, or external events". Basel II adopted this definition but eliminated the reference to indirect losses. By now most financial institutions have adopted the above definition of operational risk with relatively minor modifications.

Basel II has gone well beyond minimum regulatory capital for operational risk. It has dwelt considerably on policy, oversight and management of operational risk. Basel Committee on Banking Supervision (2003a), also known as the sound practices document, enumerates 10 high level basic principles of operational risk management. The establishment of a central operational risk function independent of business units is a requirement of governance under Basel II. Three of the principles in the Basel sound practices document deal with oversight by the board of directors and executive management. This has led banks to create enterprise wide operational risk policy, independence statements and a mechanism of reporting and escalating operational risk issues to the Board.

Basel II has partially coincided with heightened emphasis on corporate governance and regulatory compliance, particularly in the US. In terms of management of risks and controls, assessment of the quality of controls and in terms of the nature of implementation, many regulatory provisions including the Sarbanes–Oxley Act and means of corporate governance have a lot in common with the standards and concepts set forth in the advanced approach for operational risk in Basel II. Perhaps as a result of this, elements of operational risk in Basel II seem to have taken a life of their own for all publicly traded financial institutions, irrespective of whether they have to comply with Basel II. While varying in where the most emphasis is placed, the new operational risk management in financial institutions, large and not so large, have many things in common with the provisions of Basel II and are enterprise-wide in application.

The incorporation of internal control and business environmental factors required under Basel II has taken shape in two almost distinct components. The first, periodic *risk and control self-assessment* can be considered contemporaneous-looking; the second, *key risk indicators* (KRI) can be considered forward-looking. Readers are no doubt familiar with self-assessment. Basel II standardises the definition of operational event categories across all functions of a financial institution, thus facilitating benchmarking, and promotes root cause analysis, which enables prevention of future operational events. Conceptually, KRIs are leading or predictive indicators of potential future operational events and losses and thus can provide early warning for taking action. Intelligent prevention of operational loss events clearly supplements operational efficiency.

But more than that, implementation of a process-focused enterprise wide operational risk system along the lines of Basel II has the promise of improving operational efficiency. The concepts of key risk indicators and risk and control self-assessment system in general, have similarities with statistical process control in industrial firms, variously known as total quality management propagated by Edward Deming and Six Sigma initiative, introduced by Motorola and popularised by General Electric. If the operational risk management system is built with operational processes as the lowest building block, then the information collected from such an enterprise-wide system can be used for process improvement and process re-engineering (as well as management of operational risk), thus improving efficiency. These concepts have been known and applied in enlightened manufacturing companies for decades (see Shepard-Walwyn, 2004, for details). A unified conceptual treatment of key risk indicators and key performance indicators can be found in Vinella (2004).

A couple of recent studies from Wharton School, University of Pennsylvania provide another motivation for measurement and management of operational risk in financial institutions along the lines of Basel II. The first one (see Cummins *et al* 2005) shows that reported operational loss event has a significant negative impact on stock price (market value) on the institution both for banking and insurance companies. The size of market value loss of an institution is *several* times the operational loss reported by the institution. The second one (see Cummins and Wei 2006) shows that there is spillover effect, in terms of stock price drop, on other institutions in the industry. Of course, the average effect is much smaller than the average market value erosion of the institution in which the event happened. Thus, investors perceive the report of a large operational event as *symptomatic* of poor operational risk management and controls not only in the institution in question but, to some extent, throughout the industry.

Financial institutions need to *signal* their effectiveness in operational risk management and control. This minimises potential market value erosion when an operational event ends up happening, unfortunately that is, as a result of randomness even when operational risk management and effectiveness of controls in the institution are of high quality. Qualifying for advanced measurement approaches (AMA) of Basel II is one such signal. It is likely to be an effective signal for institutions that are not required to be under Basel II (eg, insurance companies, non-bank financial companies, medium-sized banks in the US).

BASEL II, DATA REQUIREMENTS AND ANALYTICS BASED STRATEGY

Basel II emphasises data-based statistical measurement of risk. While the data requirements of Basel II are significant, the Accord is *not simply* a data and information systems exercise. The Basel II requirement to rate similar loans the same way across the organisation calls for a consistent platform enterprise-wide. The Basel II requirement to link risk ratings to loan performance calls for a mapping to loan accounting systems and preserving history of data on relevant fields. The most efficient way to achieve this is perhaps to have a *data warehouse*. Building a data warehouse in a financial institution with multiple systems, at various stages of customisation, is very expensive. But it is generally less than the cost of building a customer relationship management (CRM) platform. In the last few years there has been a flurry of large investments in CRM solutions by financial institutions and while some have been successful, there have been many financial services "CRM disasters" (see Rigley 2003). Untill recently, the information content of most CRM solutions did not even include some vital risk parameters (eg, economic capital on a loan) related to the customer. Combining the data-warehouse type objectives of Basel II and those of CRM provides a much stronger business case for the technology and personnel investment required.[3] This will be true for those institutions contemplating CRM investment and also for those who need to revamp their recently implemented CRM solutions. Note that this is generally the *single largest item* of expenditure in Basel II implementation and a stronger business case helps in getting Board approval.

Viewing Basel II as a regulatory requirement or tax will invariably lead to an investment that satisfies only the minimum data requirements. Of course, it will generally lead to a significant improvement in risk management in the institution. But for most banks and all non-bank financial institutions it will perhaps not provide actual significant relief in the capital they currently hold. This means that while the bare minimum investment will still be very considerable, the institution will not be able to reap all the benefits. The latter come from what may be termed *"analytics based strategy"*. It includes optimising portfolio (credit) risk, maximising response rates while minimising customer risk during solicitation, designing and delivering in-demand and profitable new products based on customer information and risk assessment, increasing number of products consumed by a relationship or customer, etc.

1   However, it is commonly believed that competitive pressures will force many other banks to opt-in, particularly when the investor community starts demanding the same level of transparency from all publicly traded banks as those provided by the mandatory banks.
2   This was the original intention though in some jurisdictions, Pillar 2 requirements and some extraneous considerations outside of Basel II, this may not turn out to be the case.
3   In many ways, a data warehouse may be considered a pre-requisite to a CRM platform.

REFERENCES

Basel Committee on Banking Supervision, 2001, *The New Basel Capital Accord*, Consultative Document, January (CP2).

Basel Committee on Banking Supervision, 2003a, *Sound Practices for the Management and Supervision of Operational Risk*, February.

Basel Committee on Banking Supervision, 2003b, *The New Basel Capital Accord*, Consultative Document, April (CP3).

Basel Committee on Banking Supervision, 2004a, *The New Basel Capital Accord*, Consultative Document, January.

Basel Committee on Banking Supervision, 2004b, *International Convergence of Capital Measurement and Capital Standards: A Revised Framework*, June.

Basel Committee on Banking Supervision, 2006, *International Convergence of Capital Measurement and Capital Standards: A Revised Framework Comprehensive Version*, June.

Cummins, J. D., C. Lewis, and R. Wei, 2005, "The Market Value Impact of Operational Loss Events For US Banks and Insurers", Working Paper, The Wharton School, University of Pennsylvania, September.

Cummins, J. D. and R. Wei, 2006, "Financial Sector Integration and Information Spillovers: Effects of Operational Risk Events on US Banks and Insurers", Working Paper, The Wharton School, University of Pennsylvania, March.

Kofman, J., 2004, *The Benefits of Basel II and the Path to Improved Financial Performance*, Moody's KMV Company.

KPMG International, 2004, *Basel II: A Worldwide Challenge for the Banking Business.*

Rigley, J., 2003, *Overcoming CRM Failure in Financial Services: What's Not Working*, CRMGuru.com, February.

Shepheard-Walwyn, T., 2004, "KRI VaR, Lessons from Manufacturing for the Financial Services Industry," *The RMA Journal*, Special Edition, May, pp 48–51.

Vinella, P., 2004, "A Foundation for KPI and KRI", *Operational Risk*, **5(11)**, pp 38–42.

Webb, A., 1999, "Controlling Operational Risk", *Derivatives Strategy*, **4(1)**, pp 17–21.

Index